MW01592869

Selling Your Practice

*The Essential Guide to Successfully
Transition Out Of Dentistry*
Dr. David Phelps, DDS

ISBN 978-1-7332345-2-8 (paperback)

Dedicated to:

The incredible members of Freedom Founders who are bravely ditching the traditional financial model they were taught by society, creating financial Freedom for themselves and their families, and discovering their "next" together. You inspire me!

Table of Contents

Introduction

"Toto, I have a feeling we're not in Kansas anymore," said Dorothy to her dog after surviving the tornado in the Wizard of Oz.

Many of our colleagues in the health professions, certainly in the dental industry, might utter similar words today. If you had been asleep for the last decade and had just woken, you would discover that the dental profession landscape has changed substantially.

For better or worse? That depends. It depends on who you are and how well you have been able to adapt to the changes and maintain a viable and profitable practice.

Selling a practice (or any business for that matter) is complex. There are a multitude of considerations and decisions that have to be made in determining the when, the how, and the who of selling your practice. Unfortunately, few give much thought to selling or exiting until the day they decide they want to sell. Or, in some cases, _must_ sell (due to disability, death or fatigue).

For the reader's benefit, I have not only incorporated my advice and observations, but those of several other experienced consultants and thought leaders in the dental industry. It is prudent and my recommendation to not rely solely on the advice of one person in making a decision as crucial as selling one's practice. Start with seeking guidance from buyer coaches or advisors and offer to pay them a fee. From there, seek advice and counsel from several other people (tax, legal, and financial) who can provide different perspectives on critical issues for you to consider as a seller. It's best to organize an advisory "team". Choose wisely as they will influence your future. Don't shortcut this – it will cost you if you do.

The benefit of planning a practice sale or partial practice sale is strategic in many ways. Selling any business usually does not happen quickly but this allows for the conversations and discovery process of the planning to build a much clearer picture for the owner and his or her spouse. This clarity usually gives the few hardworking professionals assurance to believe it is okay to sell earlier than age 60, 65, or 70.

As of this book's publishing, we are enjoying the 8th year of a bull run economic market that grew out of the Great Recession of 2008. Interest rates are historically low (the lowest point in the past 40 years) and credit (loans) are widely available to those who have good credit and a good business or business model for acquisition. Open and accessible financing is what drives a sound economy. But take that financing away, and a recession with higher unemployment, foreclosures, and business failures ensues. Economic conditions can always change within a short amount of time. This makes the world we live in unpredictable. We can't change that.

We live in a very volatile time, where predictability is not a word used often. You have to be willing and able to "take what the market gives you" at any given time. And that's not easy for those of us who like to plan.

A change in the economy, a market reset or recession, or a rise in interest rates can change the selling environment overnight. You can't plan more than three years, if that, with any real predictability or certainty as to what conditions will be like for selling a practice at a later date.

If you are not currently in a position to sell your practice, then focus on your best business model. This means, besides being the clinician-owner, wearing all of the other hats such as human resources, marketing, operations, and financial metrics. Focus on being as lean and mean as possible while still delivering the quality and value that you desire for your patient base.

If you are five years or more from selling all or part of your practice, then you must become crystal clear on the practice model that will carry you forward (much of the remainder of this book outlines those models and how you might determine which is best for you). Lack of clarity and intention in your practice model could be not only very frustrating but also devastating to your financial security.

The Associate Practice model:

The pure associate model is a complicated model to run consistently. Associates, with no financial skin in the game and no option or pathway to ownership, are just like any other employee – as long as it works for them, they will stay. But as soon as there is a better opportunity or they are dissatisfied for any reason, they will give notice and leave. I call this the "associate turnstile."

The fact that it is challenging, if not impossible, to retain long-term associates in practice (outliers do exist), means that this model of "practice growth or expansion" is hazardous for the dentist-owner. Building out the physical facility and staff/labor component to support the associate(s) falls entirely on the owner dentist. As long as the associate is a producing member of the team, all is good. The day the associate is gone, the owner dentist has to scramble to deal with maintaining the office production, patient demand, and practice profitability.

I am aware of numerous situations where associates left the owner dentist in a bind that took the better part of a year or more to fill successfully. Not only is this model stressful, it often doesn't make long-term financial sense. To expand the production of the practice, the owner needs to have a "path to ownership" and trial partnership agreements in place for the associate.

Most people (and dentists) make decisions (or fail to make decisions) without the ability to assess the opportunities as well as the risks fully. Overall, dentists tend to be more risk-averse; that's good for a professional career that deals in micro millimeters, measuring three times before cutting, etc. But on significant life or career decisions, this high degree of analysis often causes paralysis and the procrastination of decisions until it forces a reactive or defensive action. That's never a desirable position.

Considerations you need to make regarding when, how and to whom you sell:

- Do you want a "walk-away" sale, or are you open to or even desire to continue to practice after your sale without the ownership responsibilities (as an associate)?
- Can you handle the loss of control when you sell and stay on as an associate vs. remaining independent until the day you sell?
- Do you have a propensity toward being the clinician (the technical work) or more focused on the business (CEO/owner)?
- What are your lifestyle desires, especially in terms of time and flexibility of your schedule?
- Do you have a "next" to replace your career in your timeline to exit?
- What is your financial situation – current debt load, lifestyle, the profitability of your current practice?
- How adaptable are you to change? (If you sell and stay on as an associate for more than a few months?).

- What is your geographical location in terms of competition, degree of insurance and corporate dentistry proliferation?
- What is your practice model – are you fee for service, boutique affluent, hybrid FFS and PPO or primarily PPO?

Who's your buyer?
- Traditional "my first practice" young graduate, associate or a relocation dentist. (The selling doctor cannot plan on staying on as an associate more than a few months after the sale as the buying doctor will not have enough production to maintain the financials and support you at the same time.)
- A small group of private dentists – generally, the selling doctor is required to stay for some time (a year or longer).
- A large group of private dentists (with other practices) – same as above. Buyers will want the selling doctor to remain for a final period (years) of time.
- DSO or corporate – seller will be required to stay for three years or more. DSO's or corporations will almost always pay a higher multiple of net profit for the practice than the other buyers as this buyer

is not limited by a bank or institutional financing constraints (they have access to private equity).

Important consideration regarding Private sale (to the individual dentist-buyer):

- Your market (number of potential buyers) continues to decrease not due to lack of numbers of available dentists, but due to the massive debt load that the majority of young dentists carry out of school. As practice values increase above $1M, the pool of potential private buyers who are financially capable of buying that practice continues to decrease. $1M and under practice values have a higher likelihood of being financeable for an individual buyer.

While this book is not a comprehensive tome on the subject, it will raise key issues and cause you to gather more information and advice from your advisor team.

To your freedom,

David

Chapter 1 - The Retirement Window

The Future of Dentistry and a Unique Window of Opportunity for Savvy Practice Owners

Since the early 2000s, we have seen countless stories about industries being disrupted.

We've seen new technologies destroy the video rental industry and leave bookstores teetering on the brink. We've seen mobile, price-comparison technology lead to consolidation in pharmacies, shuttering many regional ones and making it almost impossible for independent pharmacies to compete. And we've seen outside investments change the dynamics of industries like manufacturing and technology. The speed of this disruption is even more worrisome. A LOT can shift in a decade. Created just eleven years ago, AirBnB is wreaking havoc on the established hospitality industry, forcing juggernauts like Marriot, Hyatt, and Hilton to double down and redesign their business models. In just ten years, Uber and Lyft have managed to threaten taxicabs with extinction. Almost all industries are facing what I call the "Amazon" effect: increased commoditization coupled with skyrocketing consumer expectations.

Over the past decade, we've seen the same disruptive trends impact the healthcare industry, including dentistry.

Disruption and The Dental Industry

With an aging population, healthcare and dentistry have begun to experience tremendous growth in demand -- which makes them big targets of disruption from technology, corporate consolidation, and outside investments. Several new technologies have disrupted the dental world, including at-home orthodontics and teeth whitening. While the quality of at-home treatment alternatives might be questionable when compared to in-office care, there's no denying that many consumers are willing to accept lower-quality treatment for significant cost savings.

Historically, many of the medical service industries (i.e. dentistry, veterinary, optometry, pharmacy) could operate with a great degree of inefficiency. In the face of rising consumerism, those inefficiencies have become the target of "big money." Corporate consolidations—in the form of Dental Support Organizations, or DSOs—have taken advantage of the inefficiencies in the old mom-and-pop type of dental practices that once thrived despite varying degrees of overhead. Corporate owned (as in the case of Heartland, Pacific, and Aspen) or private, DSOs grow by acquiring practices, centralizing management, and leveraging their power to create large practices, which may be fee-for-service (FFS), preferred provider organization (PPO), or combined FFS and PPO practices (hybrid models).

When DSOs take over, they immediately reduce costs and boost profitability through centralizing management, HR, and marketing, as well as by implementing best practices developed across all their offices. They also leverage corporate guarantees and combined purchasing power to negotiate favorable lease terms and cut beneficial deals with suppliers, manufacturers, and insurance companies.

Private equity firms have also turned their attention to the dental industry, leveraging cheap Wall Street money along with their existing influence and relationships with insurance companies and dental suppliers. This focus will continue as long as Wall Street money remains cheap and dental industry growth is still attractive.

While these factors would create significant disruption at any time, the financial situation of dental school graduates leaves many unable to start or buy an existing practice for many years. Weighed down by between $250,000 and $500,000 in student loans, these new dentists need a guaranteed salary and benefits to pay off their debt, making them a perfect fit for the corporate model.

As long as technological advancements, corporate consolidations, and outside investment dollars flood the dental market, this disruption will only accelerate.

However, the current trend of corporate consolidations and acquisitions of independent practices will likely not last forever. Specifically, when corporate entities grow large enough, it stops being worth their time to search for independent practices and conduct the due diligence of acquiring them. Only purchasing larger organizations can have enough of an impact on their financials to make it worth their time. Right now, corporate is taking the "low hanging fruit" of acquisitions, but at some point, it becomes more efficient and cost effective to move to a de novo "startup" model. Outside investments will also slow down and even stagnate, as the natural deceleration of growth in the healthcare and dental industry will cause private equity and venture capital dollars to look elsewhere.

In the dental world, we are in the middle of a unique period of time during which technology, consolidations, and outside investments are in a state of frenzy that is likely to last until sometime between 2023 and 2025. At that point, the current trend will likely morph into a different model, thus ending the current "window of opportunity" to sell private practices at top dollar.

Like independent pharmacies or brick-and-mortar retailers trying to survive today, independent practices will have to navigate a marketplace that is turning against them. As reimbursements continue to decrease, expect fierce, unwavering competition from bigger, stronger corporate and private-equity-backed practices.

The Future of the Dental Industry

We can learn a lot about what the dental industry will look like from other industries, such as pharmacy, retail, and taxicabs.

Take the pharmacy industry: a changing regulatory environment, consolidation, new technologies (including PillPack by Amazon), and low reimbursement rates have made it increasingly difficult to run independent pharmacies profitably.

While much of the attention of the changing pharmacy market has focused on rising drug prices to consumers, multiple reports and surveys show that a large percentage of independent pharmacies across the country are struggling to survive, slashing hours, cutting staff, and even closing their doors in large numbers.

Independent pharmacies are unlikely to disappear completely; however there's no denying it will be much harder for independent pharmacists in the future. They will be competing against well-funded competitors with purchasing power and the ability to set prices they cannot match.

Independent dental practices will face similar challenges. If they try to use the traditional practice model, they will struggle to compete against practices backed by the DSOs of private equity firms. The hybrid private model may cease to exist: Running an FFS and PPO with a solo or small group practice will not be viable, as the model is too close to how practices backed by DSOs or private equity operate. Independent dentists will have to charge patients hundreds or even thousands of dollars more per year--

which will make it tough to keep existing patients, much less acquire new ones. Corporate offices will eventually drive small, hybrid private practices out of business.

The only way for hybrid, independent practices to survive is if they change their business model, so they are not competing for the same patients. One option is to switch to a Medicaid practice, which is a high-efficiency business model. For practices where the demographics include a large pool of Medicaid patients, this could work, as long as the government doesn't reduce entitlement spending.

Another option is to convert to a concierge or boutique private practice. Although demographics will still be important to consider before converting to this model, it could be a viable option for a private dentist with a higher level of clinical skills located in a more affluent area. Branding and practice experience will be very important with this model. You must know how to market and build authority as a high-end practice, which means understanding what affluent people want and building an office experience to match. There will always be people who can and will pay for access to the best dental experiences and who will not accept mediocre care.

Medicaid and concierge or boutique practices each present challenges and opportunities. Because they do not compete for the patients corporate practices have their eyes on, they will survive, but only with the owner/operator's focused intention.

Opportunity Within the Uncertainty

While the uncertainty of disruption can be scary, savvy business owners who take advantage of opportunities during strategic moments can be big winners.

For example, while most people know Blockbuster as the company Netflix disrupted to the point of bankruptcy, many people don't know that Blockbuster declined the opportunity to acquire Netflix in the spring of 2000 for $50 million. Less than a decade later, Blockbuster filed for bankruptcy protection. Netflix, on the other hand, grew to be worth more than $125 billion as of September 2019.

Additionally, in the mid-2000s, the social media world experienced a similar confluence of technology, consolidation, and outside investment. While many small entities disappeared during that period, the owners of the first successful social network, Myspace, took advantage of the hot market to sell their company to Rupert Murdoch's News Corp. for $585 million in 2005. That price-tag is notable for many reasons, although none more than the fact that News Corp. resold Myspace to Specific Media for only $35 million six years later. While many factors played into such a steep loss, there's no denying the owners of Myspace won the transaction by identifying and taking advantage of a unique exit window. Like dentistry today, their industry was flooded with technology acceleration, consolidation opportunities, and outside investment dollars in 2005.

In the dental world, independent practices are in some ways very similar to Myspace in 2005: although the model is currently working, they are facing increased competition and substantial disruption. That's the dental environment today. And that can feel scary. But the good news is your environment does not not determine your outcome. Your *response* to the environment determines your outcome. And you have options.

We've already discussed two options to position yourself against the corporate practice takeover: Medicaid and concierge/boutique practices. A potential third option would be the formation of private group practices. This requires dentists (who are traditionally slow to collaborate or "partner") to learn a new skill-set. Although this takes a lot of upfront work to put together sustainably, it is certainly a viable option for entrepreneurial, collaborative practitioners.

A fourth option would be to take advantage of the unique window of opportunity when DSOs, private equity firms (and even private buyers) are looking to acquire private practices for top dollar. This option is the primary subject of this book. It is the right fit for many practice owners who are planning on transitioning out of dentistry in three to five years, as they can now get top dollar while ensuring the practice will live on for their employees and patients. A big liquidity event can allow owners to focus only on what they love moving forward, whether that's remaining in practice without the worries of running a business or cashing out and finding their next career move.

But this window of opportunity will not stay open forever. In addition to acquiring independent practices, DSOs are already shifting to starting their own--which is attractive because they can dictate the culture and operations from day one. As their impact on the market shutters independent practices, DSOs will have little incentive to continue acquiring practices for top dollar. They will be able to open new practices for less money and just wait for the independent practices to close.

The bottom line is that now is a critical moment for practice owners who are interested in selling their practice for maximum return: For those who are not ready to leave for good, they can sell and stay on, focusing on dentistry; for those who are ready to build a legacy beyond dentistry, the financial security of a sale offers a unique opportunity to find their next season without financial pressure.

Using This Unique Opportunity to "Find Your Next"

What would you do with your focus and energy if you were financially free? What would you do if you could take advantage of this unique window of time to cash out while money is flooding the dental industry?

In the Freedom Founders mastermind group that I lead, I am passionate about helping dentists get their financial platform in place through alternative investments.

The purpose of my mission is to help dentists build wealth, independent of their practice, so they have more freedom to pursue their true passion: Some will choose to continue to practice on their own terms; others choose to leave dentistry once they can fund their desired lifestyle through alternative investments.

Too many dentists only continue to practice because they need the money. But it doesn't matter how much money you make, if you *must* continue to practice to sustain your lifestyle, you *are not* free. You might take nice vacations, live in a big house, and drive a luxury car. But you are not *truly* free.

I help dentists build the financial foundation to have freedom and options. If they continue to practice, it's by choice, not obligation. If they choose to move on, I help them do what I call "finding your next."

There has never been a better time to cash out and make the most of your life investment. No matter what path you choose, you have many options, and independent practice owners who act quickly can achieve true financial freedom.

The best news is, there has never been a better time to "find your next." No matter what age you retire, most enterprising dentists aren't ready to just sit on the couch, play golf or lounge on the beach for the rest of their lives. We have other passions we want to explore. We want to continue to be productive members of society. We just might not want to practice dentistry anymore.

So what do we do with all this opportunity? Simple. We choose. For perhaps the first time since graduating from dental school, we have a short window of time during which we can decide what we want to do with the next phase of our lives without having to worry about financial pressure.

Today, the sky's the limit. We can connect with people around the world easier, faster, and cheaper than ever before. We can establish ourselves as influencers in areas we're passionate about, through publishing, speaking, and networking opportunities that didn't exist even a few years ago. We have unprecedented access to information that makes investing in real estate and other alternative investments easier than ever.

No matter what we want to transition into, we have tremendous resources at our fingertips. We have an unprecedented opportunity to maximize the equity sale of our practices—like Myspace did in 2005—and establish ourselves in the next phase of our lives without financial pressure. Or, we could wait, do nothing, and navigate the coming dental industry environment. Perhaps we will still be able to cash out during that time, but buyers might only be willing to pay a fraction of what they are willing to pay today.

Bottom line, this is a choice. You either make it by intention, or it will happen by default. The latter is usually a poor option. What would you do during the next phase of your life if you could lift all the financial pressure from your shoulders?

How This Book Can Help You

I strongly believe in the power of expertise. I believe we make better decisions when we get trustworthy advice from the right authorities:

That's why I wrote this book and why I structured it the way I did. Specifically, I reached out to leading experts in the dental industry who can speak to exit strategies, and the transition out of practicing and into the next phase of life. I interviewed each of them about the unique window of time we're in and how *you* can cash out of your practice and find your next before the window closes. To help you make the best decision for *your* practice and *your* next, I gathered and interviewed the best minds in the dental industry for you.

Meet Your Experts

Imagine sitting in a conference room with a team of experts willing to share the wisdom they acquired from helping hundreds or even thousands of other practice owners. What would you ask them? What would you want to know? How empowering would it feel to leave that room knowing you had a team of experts invested in helping you make the best decision for yourself and your family?

The rest of this book is your virtual conference room. Around the table are Dr. Brady Frank, Dr. Dustin Burleson, Dr. Mike Abernathy, Dr. Paul Goodman, Tim Lott (CPA), and Jerry Jones (Business Expert), all dentists and/or consultants passionate about helping other dentists improve their business and personal lives. Each of them has unique experience and perspective on how you can take advantage of the retirement window to cash out and transition to your next, either inside or outside of the dental industry.

Dr. Brady Frank helps solo dental practitioners utilize DSO investments. In addition to talking about the pros and cons of cashing out through a DSO model, Brady and I also discuss the importance of being productive during the next season of life by doing something we love. We talk about how people who choose to retire without a plan in place end up feeling lost. Because this lack of direction can have a serious impact on a person's physical and mental wellbeing, Brady agreed that it's important for all of us to continue to be productive, especially if we take advantage of the retirement window to cash out of dentistry.

Dr. Dustin Burleson has a unique, hands-on perspective about selling dental practices. Dustin and I discuss how most business owners don't start planning their exit soon enough. Ideally, for Dustin, planning should start on day one of your practice, but at a minimum he says it takes two to three years to prepare for an optimal exit. As one of the best exit strategists around, he gives tremendous insight into the minds of practice purchasers that can help you get top dollar. He also details a unique exit strategy that can help you substantially reduce tax obligations from selling your practice.

Dr. Mike Abernathy is the founder of Summit Practice Solutions, which helps dental practice owners grow their practices and their profits. I count myself among the many people he's helped along the way, when he rescued me from my failed practice sale, so I could make my own exit from clinical dentistry. Mike and I talk about options for generating top dollar for your practice, as the pool of purchasers diminishes. Sharing his insights into preparing for the next phase of your life, he talks about how the reality of business and life has caused too many dentists to feel like they might never be able to retire. Mike's interview explores the true impact of taking advantage of the retirement window and finding your next.

Dr. Paul Goodman is one of the most active professionals in the dental industry, with extensive experience buying and selling practices on his own behalf, as well as in his capacity as a broker. Paul and I discuss how the buyer mix will be changing as the retirement window closes. For example, years ago, with more individual buyers, sales happened quickly, and the buyer would only ask the seller to stay on for a short transition period. Sales to corporate buyers tend to take a longer time. Thus, owners are wise to get started as soon as possible in preparing their practice for a sale. Paul also shares additional ways to take advantage of the retirement window, for example, through creative collaborations with other practice owners.

Tim Lott is a CPA whose unique position in the dental world puts additional perspective on the dental market.

Tim helps doctors fresh out of school and deeply in debt. As he suggests, the best way to get out of debt is to become a practice owner. He sees dentists who are three to five years out of school taking the plunge into practice ownership through leverage. With 20% down, many banks will finance a practice purchase, Tim suggests. Moreover, with DSOs often willing to pay more for practices because of their centralized management model, practice values have risen significantly. When the DSOs turn their attention elsewhere, however, Tim warns that practice value can drop again.

If you've been a member of Freedom Founders or connected with me in one way or another, you have probably met Jerry Jones. Jerry is a good friend of mine, a non-dentist business entrepreneur and marketer, who has bought, sold, or started eighteen companies over the past twenty-five years. This impressive portfolio includes the purchase of several dental practices, from the early 2000s until May 2018, when Jerry decided to step out of dental practice ownership completely. He's seen it all when it comes to buying and selling and has experience both inside and outside dentistry, which gives him valuable perspective as to how external investors look at buying practices. He shares insights into mindset, exit strategies, preparing for your next, and more.

Your team of experts covers everything you need to know about the retirement window and finding your next. You'll get advice about preparing your practice for sale, choosing what's next, and executing your plan to make the next season the best season of your life.

Are You Ready for Freedom?

The dental market landscape is changing. Today, there is a critical window of opportunity to sell your private practice for top dollar. But that window is closing. The longer you wait to take advantage of the unique opportunity to cash out, become financially free, and continue dentistry or transition to something else, the more difficult it will be.

So, if you're ready to understand exactly how you can take advantage of the retirement window, my team of experts and I are here to help you.

Chapter 2 - Dr. Brady Frank

Dsos vs Ddsos and The Unseen Challenges of Exiting Your Practice

My interview with Dr. Brady Frank was fast-paced and enthusiastic -- just like Brady himself.

Dr. Brady Frank is a go-getter. He closed on his first practice the day he graduated from dental school and purchased his second only six months later. Within seven years, he owned part or all of twelve practices.

His tall, wiry frame exudes energy. His whole face smiles with enthusiasm when he talks about the different ownership and practice models he has developed. It's easy to see how this excitement spills over into his new passion -- helping other dentists structure practice ownership and management to fit their desired lifestyle.

Brady recently retired from the clinical side of dentistry to focus on helping other dentists. After selling his interests to his partners, he now focuses his time rapidly opening dental implant institutes and offering consulting services to practice owners. In 2019, Brady, having been an implant lecturer for fifteen years, has turned his attention to helping other practitioners achieve what he has achieved in the industry. Brady has helped twelve dentists open implant institutes with a number of others opening in 2020 and a waitlist of more to follow.

He now teaches the teachers. Brady finds dentists who love implants, and helps them help others do the same (all while building four or five streams of income for themselves in the process). Brady loves to invest in the next generation of dentists looking to prepare for a post-clinical dentistry career.

I want to interview Brady because he has a deep knowledge and experience helping dentists create dentist-owned service organizations (DDSOs). If you are unsure about leaving the clinical side of dentistry but want to maximize your cash flow and the value of your practice, my discussion with Brady can help.

On Preparing for Your Exit

Before diving into the nuts and bolts of transition deals, I want to begin our interview with the bigger picture. A lot of dentists have trouble exiting their practice. Even if they have the financial means to do so, they often struggle with what to do next. For decades, they have tied their identity to their profession. This causes many dentists to stay in clinical practice way too long, even after they burn out. They want to exit, but they fear what they will do after dentistry. If they do get out without preparing, they feel lost.

Because Brady has helped so many dentists navigate the transition out of clinical practice and into teaching or other sources of cash flow, I take a few minutes to talk with him about his observations, especially what he has seen work well.

Brady's eyes light up as he dives right in.

"It's a strange thing. Dentists who don't develop interests outside of dentistry will likely just keep working and working for their entire lives."

That's the danger of thinking about "retirement" in the traditional sense. When practitioners leave clinical dentistry and the meaning that their profession has provided for so many years, they lose their drive. As their mind tends to slow down, their health tends to go downhill, too. Sometimes, the quality of their life declines quickly. It's not what many people assume when they think about retirement, but it often works out that way, Brady explains.

Instead, practice owners should take time to identify something they want to move *into* after retiring from clinical dentistry: their "next." They should develop interests, income and purpose outside of dentistry that can become their focus when they retire.

This might sound familiar to members of my Freedom Founders community. In Freedom Founders, we talk about using alternative investments to fund and create annuity income outside of dentistry and using that financial independence to discover and transition into your next phase of life.

Preparing for your exit and moving into a new phase of life that gets you excited is critical because there's no one-size-fits-all retirement plan for dentists. Some dentists want to leave clinical dentistry entirely. Others want to practice part-time. Some want to move into alternative practice ownership to develop multiple streams of income. Others want to develop income and purpose completely outside of the dental industry.

No matter what your goal is, there is a way to make your dream a reality. From Brady's perspective, in addition to finding private buyers and DSOs, practice owners should consider using a DDSO model to maximize cash flow and professional flexibility.

Transition Options

To help you understand your options during this unique window of time, I ask Brady to talk briefly about the current buyer pool for practices.

Brady and I discuss five primary ways doctors transition out of practices:

- private sales to other dentists
- adding equity partner dentists while cutting down their time commitments
- hiring associates to take over clinical work
- cashing out with a DSOs or Private Equity investor, and
- forming or joining forces with a DDSO

Here's what Brady has to say about each of these options.

Private Sales to Dentists

Historically, many dentists transitioned out of their practices by selling to newer dentists, through a walk-away sale, a sale with a short transition period, or a sale that results in the seller working as an associate for the new owner. Many walk-away sales happen through brokers who match buyers with sellers for a fee.

Selling a practice and staying on as an associate is often a choice made by doctors who get tired of doing all the work it takes to run a practice but who are not ready to completely retire from dentistry. They just don't want to work as hard. For them, working two days a week is a great option. While this can work well for some, Brady warned that there is often a major drawback to selling a practice to a private buyer—not a DSO—and continue working as an associate.

The challenge in selling to a younger dentist is that the seller loses the leadership status in the office with the team members; as an associate, they're not running the operations anymore. That shift in dynamic can be a blow to one's self-esteem and often leads to the seller leaving the practice and starting fresh as an associate at another practice.

Adding Equity Partner Dentists

A second option for doctors wanting to reduce their responsibilities without leaving dentistry is to add younger doctors as minority owners in their practice.

With this structure, the older doctor maintains leadership status while cutting down his or her clinical days. Brady has seen doctors continue under this structure for up to ten years without the awkward reversal of a long-time owner becoming an employee with no authority. This dynamic also works well for the younger dentists who want to ease into practice ownership with a more stable structure than a complete change in leadership. In that regard, it could open up the buyer pool to include doctors who want to get into practice ownership but who are not ready to buy an entire practice.

Brady says this structure works really well for doctors who just want to cut back from a leadership and financial perspective. In addition to avoiding the awkward leadership transition, this structure allows doctors to maintain an equity position and continue to profit from the practice. This structure also positions the practice to grow with the addition of another doctor. Thus, although the doctor would reduce his or her equity position, the additional profits generated from added production could offset some or all of the reduction of ownership.

In addition to yielding greater time freedom for the senior doctor, this model also builds in a transition pathway as a form of insurance should the senior doctor become unable to maintain an active treatment role or simply want to accelerate their total exit from the practice.

Adding Associates

Brady briefly touched on the option of adding associates to take over clinical work. The goal in these transactions is for the doctor to transition some or all of the clinical work to the associate while maintaining full ownership of the practice.

While adding associates sounds good in theory, the reality is it doesn't often result in doctors actually being able to cut back. It is often only a temporary addition and usually introduces more management issues and stress as your team grows. Without a path to ownership, most associates are not motivated to be as engaged in the practice as the owner would desire.

Thus, if your goal is to grow significantly, generate multiple streams of income, or cut back on the time you dedicate to your practice, adding associates will not likely be ideal.

But the grim assessment doesn't seem to dampen Brady's enthusiasm for a moment.

"I wish dental transitions were as cut and dried as real estate... but they are NOT."

Brady laughs heartily. I smile knowingly.

"That's why I do real estate."

"Yep... You might need to write a chapter about that," Brady quips with a grin. We quickly refocus on the next topic at hand, DSOs.

Selling to a DSO

It's no secret DSOs are buying private practices right now, according to Brady. He sees them generally paying cash for practices, although they use up to 20% seller financing. When DSOs buy a practice, they often ask the seller to stay on for two to five years as a salaried employee. This has become a very popular structure for doctors who want a big cash infusion and reduced operational responsibilities while continuing to work in the practice in a position of authority for a few years.

(Let me add a note of caution here: when negotiating with a potential DSO buyer, be sure to perform a high level of research and due diligence on their track-record after the sale. How does the culture change? What about staff who might become disgruntled with the change in ownership? Could you, the seller, remain as an associate in your former practice where you no longer call the shots?)

If you want to be completely out of dentistry, this might not be the perfect fit, as you will likely have to work for a few years. However, on the upside, it does provide the opportunity for a cash infusion and fewer obligations for a few years while you build into the next phase of life.

Brady warns that DSO has become a buzz-word in the dental industry, which has caused some confusion about what it really means. The typical DSO is an investor- or corporate-owned organization that provides management and other services, using a structure that helps investors get around the regulations governing the corporate practice of dentistry: the clinical entity, owned by a dentist licensed to practice in the state, enters into a series of management agreements to allow the DSO to profit from the operations of the practice.

Selling to or Creating a DDSO

The main structural difference between a DSO and a DDSO is that DDSOs are owned and operated by private practice doctors who get together to form a group practice, often with multiple locations and additional streams of income. While DDSOs fall under the same DSO umbrella from a technical perspective, they're a bit different from an operational perspective.

One nice thing about DDSOs, Brady says, is that there is no corporate practice law to get around. You don't need multiple entities and management agreements to structure them in a compliant manner.

There's a lot more flexibility because they are owned by dentists and do not have to follow a strict investment profile that governs the operations of many large DSOs.

For example, many DSOs are not interested in owning real estate. They are "management companies," so their model involves leasing real estate for their practices. In contrast, DDSOs often own the real estate associated with the practices they run. Thus, a DDSO can generate additional value through property appreciation and certainty of real estate costs.

Additionally, because DDSOs are often formed by a number of doctors joining together to create a larger practice with centralized management, each doctor tends to reduce his or her management burden. That frees the doctors up to combine forces and create additional revenue streams, such as conducting consulting or training for other dentists or acquiring additional real estate or dental practices.

One significant benefit of DDSOs is how open they tend to be with each other. It's a true joint-venture in most cases, Brady explained, unlike DSOs, which often hide their systems and processes from the doctors inside the practices. The doctors working together within a DDSO typically share their experiences and work together. DDSOs also keep practices being run by dentists and not outside corporations.

The upside of a DDSO is hard to deny, especially because of the flexibility it offers. Brady shared an example of a dentist who was the owner and founder of a DDSO in the Midwest, we'll call him "Dr. P". Dr. P was vice president of clinical operations of Heartland Dental before a private equity company invested heavily in Heartland. Dr. P left Heartland and formed his DDSO.

Between March 2018 and September 2018, Dr. P used his DDSO to acquire twenty-seven practices in six states and planned to acquire another twenty by the end of 2020. Dr. P takes full advantage of the flexibility DDSOs offer, adding several additional streams of income. He is also intentional about real estate ownership.

The Changing Landscape for Solo Practitioners

Brady emphasizes that if you're a solo practitioner and want to be out of clinical practice in the next five years, it's never been easier than today. You have significantly more options than ever before. There are many types of buyers out there and multiple exit strategies available.

However, if you're not ready to transition out of your practice in the next five years, the landscape will be changing, and you must prepare now for that change. Brady referred to the medical market as an example of how the entire health industry is changing, insofar as most medical practitioners have been consolidated and aggregated into hospital corporations. Others have formed private medical group practices that also work in hospital environments. Because the private medical groups have made it very difficult for solo practitioners, today solos are more likely to operate as a group, says Brady.

"You'll find groups of nineteen partner radiologists. You'll see surgery centers started with five orthopedists. They use scale and pooled resources to provide better patient experiences while making more money for themselves."

The same is going to happen with dentistry, Brady predicts. Solo practitioners, who have very little economy of scale, are going to find themselves being beat by DSOs and doctors who have joined together. Doctors who work with DSOs and DDSOs will have better lifestyles, better incomes, better ability to market their practices, among several other benefits. DSOs will continue to grow over the next several years, at least, and DDSOs will follow suit. Since there's no big growth curve up with solo practitioners, those who survive will be stagnant at best.

I agree with Brady's assessment and pointed out that it will take almost a Herculean effort to continue as a solo practitioner because of the lack of leverage. Even specialists or independent boutique practices will find it difficult because DSOs and DDSOs will be able to provide specialized *and* general treatment. The convenience of patients having a one-stop shop will make it very difficult for solo practitioners and small independent practices to compete. They might be able to do it for a few years, but it's a tough model to sustain over a couple of decades.

"It's all encompassing." Brady continues. "As a solo practitioner, you have to be the marketer, the producer, the manager, and more. Being solo is hard. It's just hard.

That's why people are looking for freedom and trying to get out."

Brady says to look no further than the doctors who bought his practice as an example of how much easier it is with group, DSO, or DDSO model. They only work thirty hours a week while solo-practitioners work longer hours under more difficult conditions.

A Changing of the Guard

The way we are trained and educated—in life, college, and dental school—is to roll up our sleeves and work harder than everyone else to succeed. We're taught to be autonomous and don't learn about collaboration because dental school isn't about collaboration:You take tests on your own and either pass or fail on your own.

But there's a changing of the guard as younger generations enter the dental industry. As Brady explains, there are a lot of jokes about millennials. People say they're not ambitious, they have an obsession with avocados, and can't be without their phones for more than a few minutes. But millennials grew up with social media, collaboration, and crowdfunding.

They are used to being connected with others and sharing things older generations never would. They basically learned to not do anything unless you do it as a group. Additionally, millennials come out of dental school with record student debt and love the security of having a steady paycheck with upside, which they can get more easily from DSOs and DDSOs than in many other models.

That's why we have so many millennials going straight into DSOs or DDSOs from dental school -- and why so many DSOs have a presence at dental schools. Millennials are much more likely to accept having 25% ownership of a practice if it comes with a steady salary and lower responsibilities. Older generations wanted 100% ownership and were willing to work and sacrifice as hard as they needed to for it.

Brady thinks this mindset shift actually favors retirement-age dentists. We now have a big pool of millennial doctors who already believe that collaborative structures are more profitable, easier on everybody, and better for achieving the lifestyle they want. As older dentists are starting to want a better lifestyle, they will have a growing pool of millennial doctors with whom to collaborate through a DDSO model or otherwise.

Choosing Your Best Option

Brady compared the countless options for practice owners to the variety in real estate investing. Some people prefer to flip houses for a quick profit. They find houses, make necessary repairs, give it a fresh coat of paint, sell it fast, and move out. If that's what you want to do, a walk-away sale might be the right fit. You'll get your money and move on with your life. It might not be the most money you can make, but you'll get a big cash infusion and be free to walk away.

Other people want to be more passive investors. They want to make a strong return without having to spend a lot of time or money managing their investment. A DSO model is similar to this. You get about 80% of your capital out and get paid to work another two to five years while the DSO takes over operational responsibilities. You get a strong return and stay minimally involved in the practice, getting paid for your clinical work but not having to be active in practice operations or creating additional income streams.

Others prefer to be more active investors to maximize their return on investment through joint ventures and other creative strategies. This is the equivalent of how

DDSO models can work, by joining forces with other dentists to create multiple streams of income. In fact, because of the flexibility, DDSOs can create the equivalent of flipping, passive, and active investments for doctors.

As Brady explains, some DDSOs pool resources to become private lenders, generating passive income in the form of earning interest on the money they lend. They can create active investment returns by building institutes and managing additional practices. They can create quick, flipping-type returns, by acquiring practices, implementing systems and processes, and selling them for profit.

For example, Dr. P (from Brady's previous example) is partnering with private practice dentists so they can step back from the managerial responsibilities and can get a lot of the upside of being connected to something bigger.

So, if a dentist wants to step away completely from clinical work over the next three to five years but also wants to stay involved in the business with significant upside, it would be smart to consider a DDSO model. They could offload the managerial side and might even enjoy dentistry a little bit longer and a little bit more.

My conversation with Brady was a whirlwind of insights. Here's my best effort at consolidating the key points:

Takeaways

- A lot of people have trouble exiting from their profession, whether dentistry or not. It's not always a matter of money—oftentimes it's a matter of not knowing what to do with themselves after they retire. Discovering what you want to do in your next phase of life helps bring clarity to your options.
- If you retire completely and do nothing with yourself, your health will start to decline. Having something productive to move into can help you stay active and healthy.
- Doctors have many options for exiting their practices. The five Brady discussed with me include:
  - private sales to other dentists
  - adding equity partner dentists while cutting down their time commitments
  - hiring associates to take over clinical work
  - cashing out with a DSOs or Private Equity investor and
  - forming or joining forces with a DDSO

- Each option has its place, but Brady believes DSOs and DDSOs tend to offer the most upside, with DDSOs being the most flexible with the most upside.
- DSOs are currently buying a lot of private practices. They make up a large portion of the current buyer pool.
- DSOs and DDSOs will put a big strain on solo practitioners. Doctors who are running a practice on their own are going to find themselves competing against DSOs and doctors who have joined together to have a better lifestyle, income, and ability to market.
- Millennials are more collaborative than older generations. They're introduced to DSOs and DDSOs in dental school and are more willing to own a part of a practice rather than the whole thing. This will increase the growth of DSOs and DDSOs and create opportunities for older doctors looking for creative ways to transition from their practice.

To listen to the audio recording of my interview with Dr. Brady Frank, go to:

www.SellingYourPracticeBook.com/Interviews

Chapter 3 - Dr. Dustin Burleson

Practical Strategies in the Face of a Changing Economic and Political Landscape

The next interview I conducted was with Dr. Dustin Burleson, of Burleson Orthodontics & Pediatric Dentistry which serves patients in four different locations throughout Missouri. Dustin might not be exiting dentistry right now, but he definitely knows a thing or two about the process of transitioning out of a practice.

Dustin is one of the most business savvy practitioners I know. He has a high-level coaching program that has helped hundreds of orthodontists massively outperform industry averages. He keeps his finger on the pulse of industry trends and has coached many of his clients through the transition process successfully.

We have worked closely together over the years. I consider Dustin to be a friend, as well as a respected colleague. I eagerly looked forward to sitting down with him to glean his insights.

The Best Time to Plant a Tree

There's an old Chinese proverb that says, "The best time to plant a tree was twenty years ago. The second-best time is now." According to Dustin, the same principle holds for preparing for your transition from wet-fingered dentist to your *next*.

The best time to start planning your exit strategy, according to Dustin, is the day you open the doors to your practice--although most practice owners do not. In fact, many of them don't start after one, five, or even ten years. Many of them only start thinking about it as they're nearing retirement, which leaves them ill-prepared.

In normal markets, delaying these preparations puts the practice owner at a big disadvantage. They might have to work longer than they want or sell their practice for less than fair market value. Fortunately, we're in the midst of a window of growth for the dental market, which means that the attention being paid to the dental market can help overcome late planning with DSO or DDSO money, giving you an opportunity to sell your practice for fair market value (and even a premium) if you start preparing your exit strategy today. After all, while the best time to plan your exit strategy was years ago, the second-best time is right now.

I want Dustin to talk more about the trends he sees in the market over the next five to ten years and how practice owners can best position themselves to take advantage of them. So I ask him to give his best advice to current practice owners.

The first thing Dustin discusses is taking time to get your financials organized, to maximize your practice value:

"If you haven't thought about your exit strategy, you need at least two to three years to prepare your practice to sell for top dollar."

Dustin continues with the quiet confidence of experience. "The main focus is ensuring your financials are clean and your profits are as solid as possible. With clean financials and solid profits, offers will be much higher. You will appear more trustworthy, and your practice will present itself as well-run."

I nod. That makes a lot of sense, I lean in as Dustin continues. "One way to achieve this is to focus two to three years to cut expenses from the practice, such as country club memberships, car leases, anything else you can get off the practice's balance sheet that is not directly attributable to the provision of services.

"Hmmm." I think. "That might be a tough pill to swallow for practitioners who have blended their lifestyle with their practice."

But Dustin is adamant. He argues that having three years of solid financials makes marketing and selling your practice much easier. You will likely get significantly higher offers from more buyers. Without it, smart buyers will sense that you're rushing your exit and take advantage of your situation. They will see they can immediately boost profits by all the unnecessary expenses they will no longer carry. Additionally, messy financials often give buyers less confidence in other parts of your practice, reducing their willingness to pay a premium out of concern that they will find other inefficiencies, or worse. In just two or three short years, you can significantly increase the value of your practice pretty easily.

In addition to cleaning up your financials, Dustin suggests getting other practice assets organized, optimized, and prepared for sale

"Make sure you know how to access and transfer the URL for your website, web hosting, phone numbers, and email management. Review and organize all agreements relating to your practice, including employment contracts, independent contractor agreements, equipment and real property leases, benefit plans, lab agreements, insurance plan contracts, practice management software agreements, and anything else that governs how you operate your practice. If you're missing any, get them in place. Having these things together gives buyers much more confidence purchasing your practice for top dollar."

Dustin explains that many doctors don't have those things in order, and it costs them a lot of money. They have independent contractors without signed non-compete agreements. They have employees without employment agreements. They have profit-sharing or bonus plans that aren't documented. They have negotiated arrangements with labs that have never been put in writing. All of these things will be discovered during the due diligence period, and when they are, the buyer will lower the price they're willing to move forward with to buy the practice.

But preparing your practice for maximum value is important even if you're not thinking of selling in the next few years. For example, clean finances and organized operations can make it easier to secure practice debt. It also makes running your practice much smoother. Even more importantly, it can help you get out of your practice without having to wait two or three years to clean things up if you need to exit more quickly, like if you hurt your back and can no longer work.

The Changing Buyer Mix for Dental Practices

While clean financials and operations are important to any buyer, they are even more important in this market given the changing nature of practice buyers.

Years ago, many practices sold to associates or solo dentists. Today, Dustin pointed to private equity and DSOs as major players in the dental market. Those types of buyers are much less likely to have a deep knowledge of practice operations before buying, in contrast with associates who work for a practice and take it over. They look for balance sheets and operations that match their investment model. If they see it, they pay top dollar. If they don't, they pay less because they think they will need to do a lot of work making the practice fit their model.

"So," I ask Dustin, "what do you think the dental market will look like, five or ten years out?"

"In five or ten years, the major players will be hospitals and larger DSOs—like Heartland Dental or Pacific Dental. We will see more group practices and DDSOs."

My mind travels back to my interview with Brady, discussing the grim future of private practice, and today's window of opportunity. Many members of Freedom Founders come from solo practices and want to sell for top dollar so they can find—and fund—their next phase of life. They need to get top dollar for their practices. What do they do? And what if they don't sell during this window? What does Dustin think about their future?

"It won't happen right away, but over the next five to ten years, dentistry will slowly churn toward group practices. In time, the only solo practices that will survive will be exceptionally high-end, fee-for-services practices. Moreover, if the politicians who are pushing for universal, single-payer healthcare get their way, it's possible for this timeline to accelerate. In fact, Bernie Sanders already included oral health in his healthcare plan."

Dustin's assessment seems to closely mirror Brady's, but the added political perspective intrigues me.

There's no doubt that broad healthcare reform is a priority with many political candidates. A lot of the discussions point to the possibility of a two-tier healthcare system in the near future. In a two-tier healthcare system, the top 5%–10% of income earners will go to high-end, fee-for-services hospitals, doctors' offices, and dental practices.

The other 90%–95% will go to someone within the federal insurance program. Practices with economies of scale in place will be much more equipped to be profitable in such a system than solo practitioners who are not able to build a high-end, fee-for-service practice that attracts wealthy patients.

In Dustin's words, a surviving solo practitioner will "need to be a super dentist." They will need to have top marketing skills, customer service skills, and clinical skills. They will need to place implants. And they will need to attract new patients from outside of traditional referral relationships because corporate dental and hospitals will not refer anything out.

The increasingly difficult landscape for solo practices makes it even more important to start cleaning up your financials and operations today, if they are not already in order. That gives you the maximum flexibility to take advantage of this unique market. If you decide to sell, you can do so for top dollar while there's a lot of money looking for practices. If you decide to acquire other practices, your clean financials can make you attractive to owners looking to do the same and support any potential borrowing needs to consummate a transaction.

Assembling Your Team

Dustin strongly advises having a trusted team on your side to structure your sale. A good attorney who knows how to do buy-sell agreements is an invaluable investment. The same is true for a CPA experienced in due diligence.

With these two professionals on your side, Dustin says you should not need to work with a practice broker. Specifically, Dustin suggests, "If you know what you're doing and have a good attorney and CPA, you can save the money you'd have to pay the broker and put it to work somewhere more useful."

Considering Alternative Exits

Dustin makes an interesting observation about the market for solo practices compared to group practices. Specifically, he suggests solo practices don't typically attract high premiums. One reason is because they are so dependent on the owner's work to make money. Another reason is because patients typically go to those solo practices based on the owner's reputation. If the owner leaves, patients might leave as well.

On the other hand, associate-run or group practices that attract new patients through marketing efforts are valued much more highly on the market, because patient relationships are much less dependent on one owner. Many patients don't even see the practice owner. So, if a private equity firm buys the practice, the risk of patients leaving is much lower. Additionally, if new patients find the practice through marketing efforts, a new owner can grow the practice by investing in those efforts. According to Dustin, these are the practices selling for a true forward multiple right now, and that'll be true for the next three to five years.

With this in mind, it raises the question of whether interested small practices who want to maximize their return should consider a two-step plan, growing through group efforts or building an associate- and marketing-driven model prior to making their exit.

Additionally, Dustin says practice owners should talk with an experienced exit strategist about other options. For example, employee stock ownership plans—or ESOPs—are an underutilized way to exit out of a business. Amazon even used an ESOP to avoid **billions** of dollars in potential taxes. An ESOP is one example of an alternative method to step away from a practice while maximizing your return.

The Impact of a Potential Recession

Finally, with a growing fear of a recession looming, many dentists wonder whether it may close the window for their exit earlier than expected.

For practices with clean financials and operations, Dustin doesn't believe it will have a significant impact on the market. If anything, Dustin suggests, there may be fewer deals, but the deals will likely be stronger for sellers because the investment profile for a strong practice will be much more attractive than other investments during a recessionary period.

As he puts it:

"If the stock market tanks, firms might have less money to spend, but firms will have to go somewhere. They will put money into a few safe equities, but dental practices will be an attractive alternative."

Thus, if a recession is indeed ahead, it is smart to prepare for your next right now.

Dustin's insights reveal more pieces of the puzzle, getting me excited to start piecing together the full picture. To do so, I decided to consult a personal mentor of mine for my next interview: the mentor who rescued me from my failed practice sale and helped me successfully exit clinical dentistry many years ago.

Takeaways

- If you haven't started planning your exit, do so now. It will help you no matter when you want to exit.
- It takes two to three years to prepare your finances and operations to sell for top dollar.
- Private equity currently has a strong interest in buying practices. In five to ten years, hospitals and DSOs will be major players for buying practices.
- Solo practitioners face an increasingly difficult road while group practices and associate-run and marketing-driven practices are becoming more attractive.

- Practice owners need a trusted team to guide them but do not need practice brokers to structure deals, if they have the right professionals in place.
- If you are a solo practitioner, consider two-step or alternative exits to maximize your return.

To listen to the audio recording of my interview with Dr. Dustin Burleson, go to:

www.SellingYourPracticeBook.com/Interviews

Chapter 4 - Dr. Mike Abernathy

Pros and Cons of Private Buyers vs Corporate Buyers

There was a lump in my throat as I hung up the phone.

This wasn't how the sale of my dental practice was supposed to go. The practice I had fought so hard to build was crumbling. I had to suit back up, take back the practice and try again. Only this time, I was determined to learn from my mistakes. To do so, I needed a mentor.

That's when Dr. Abernathy entered the scene.

Before helping me navigate my transition, Dr. Mike Abernathy already had an impressive resume in the business of dentistry. He formed Summit Practice Solutions (Summit) to help dental practice owners grow their practices and their profits. He had grown multiple practices, including a general dental practice in McKinney, Texas, which he built it into one of the largest and most profitable practices in the U.S. before exiting in 2005. He also built a portfolio of practices across the U.S., many of which were distressed at the time he acquired them. Through Summit's coaching and consulting services, he was able to streamline operations and improve those practices as an absentee owner.

In 2015, Mike also founded BEST for Dentistry to further help independent practice owners. BEST, which stands for *Building Everyone's Success Together*, advocates on behalf of independent practices with the goal of giving members the same buying power as large national corporate chains. But BEST is not only a group purchasing organization. It also gives members tools to help them provide top-quality clinical care, improve patient acquisition, and implement business strategies that help them thrive in any economy.

Dr. Abernathy speaks with humble authority. His weathered face and steady gaze gives him the aura of a no-nonsense marine commander. It's only once you get to know him that you can recognize the playful sparkle in his eyes.

With such long-term, deep experience in the dental industry, I want to get his perspective on the trends he sees in today's market for smaller, independent practices. He's eager to share.

"While decreasing, the most common type of sale remains to another doctor," he asserts confidently. "That said, selling to another doctor might not be the best fit for many practices. Additionally, not all practices are created equal when it comes to being able to be sold to another doctor."

He continues, adding more depth:

"An average practice doing $650,000 a year with a decent profit margin and a few employees is somewhat easy to sell to another doctor. It is also not as attractive to a larger corporate practice, so those sales don't tend to result in sellers receiving top dollar for their practice."

I appreciate the specific example. Mike continues...

"Banks are comfortable lending to doctors looking to buy a small practice for a low price point. A doctor can pretty easily borrow $500,000 to help them finance a $650,000 purchase only having to pay the small difference of $150,000."

But here, Mike pauses gravely.

"These transactions are decreasing, however, because many practices are producing more and more, growing them above the level at which banks are comfortable financing but not big enough for corporate dollars to pay a big premium. If a dentist is making $1 million a year, which is becoming more and more common, that practice is probably going to sell pretty close to $750,000 or $800,000. At that level, it gets harder for a buyer to secure a bank loan."

But, based on my previous interviews with Brady and Dustin, I know that practice owners have numerous alternatives to selling to other doctors, even with smaller practices. So, I ask Mike to walk us through the alternatives he has seen work best for practice owners.

Using Fractional Sales to Maximize Return on a Smaller Practice

Mike exited his practice by selling fractional shares to associates who proved themselves to be the right fit. While that helped him maximize his return, it was a lot harder and took a lot longer than a one-buyer transaction.

Selling fractional interests maximizes returns because it expands the buyer pool and makes it easier for buyers to get into practice ownership, even if they have to pay a premium on the share value.

But Mike went through *fourteen* associates before he found one who was a good fit. He needed someone who had a fire in their belly, who wanted ownership, and who wanted to grow a practice. He needed somebody who had a great self-image, great people skills, and who was already self-motivated. In Mike's experience, only a fraction of new doctors have those qualities.

It took a long time for Mike to exit through fractional ownership, even if he ended up achieving a higher return. Each associate he brought in spent fifteen to twenty-four months at his practice. Few came close to duplicating the horsepower and charisma he had that made their practice successful. He needed somebody to replace it, add to it, compensate for the things he didn't do well, and complement the existing culture. But it took him fourteen associates to find the right fit. Thus, in addition to the additional management responsibilities involved, bringing in associates isn't always a quick process for doctors looking to exit.

Additionally, until you sell all pieces of ownership, you maintain -- if not increase -- your leadership and management responsibilities. A lot of doctors who go this route are not prepared, so having someone like Mike coach can help make things much smoother. Mike also suggested selling two 50% fractions, which tends to be easier than selling smaller percentages because you only have to find two associates ready for fractional ownership.

Finally, if you want to maintain control of your practice until you sell 100% of your shares, have the practice's operating agreement make you the managing partner, that way, you're in charge even if you've sold 97% of the practice ownership. Losing control after selling 50% or more of their practice is a common—and well-founded—concern of practice owners looking to exit.

Getting to Know Corporate Buyers and DSOs

Mike finds little practical difference between corporate buyers and DSOs. Like any business, each has subtle differences in how they operate, but the big picture is similar.

While the term "DSO" has become a buzzword today, DSO's have been around since 1975. Originally the DSO model was designed so a non-dentist could own a dental practice, but it's changed because there are now a lot of doctors who want to use DSO models to run and grow their practices. Today, corporate and DSO buyers are a major player for the right practices.

"Who are these corporate buyers?" I ask.

"A lot of corporate buyers are successful dentists turned entrepreneurs who have a proven management model that has worked on a number of practices. Many times, they started out as a doctor who had a really good run with a solo practice, grown it through adding doctors, and streamlined operations to limit overhead to no more than 63%."

"How do they go from that to becoming an influential, 'corporate' buyer of other practices?"

"A lot of times, these doctors get bored doing the day-to-day stuff of running a practice that has good systems and processes in place. So, they open a second practice as a growth plan and realize running a second practice is much harder than they anticipated."

I nod vigorously. My own experience with Freedom Founders members has taught me that this is indeed true.

Mike continues:

"What they realize during the struggle is, as good as their systems were for running the first practice, what really drove the first practice was the personality, charisma, and horse-power of that original doctor—not as much by systems and protocols. They often struggle mightily with it and few doctors move beyond the second location. Many of them shut down the second location and go back to running just one."

I remember the many ways that Mike helped me build systems in my own practice before my successful transition. Mike certainly speaks from experience.

"Others don't give up on that second practice and realize they have to reconstruct their model, so they can have a strong culture and business model that will continue to work as an absentee owner. Once they get past the second one, though, they can add as many as they want."

"Wow," I think. What a gem of an insight from Mike.

One practice goes smoothly, so an entrepreneurial dentist opens another. But what works in the first practice doesn't work with the second one. However, if they adjust their model to work as an absentee owner, their growth is unlimited, and they can start looking for smaller practices to buy and adjust to their model.

When Selling to Corporate Buyers or DSOs is Not a Good Fit

In Mike's experience, founders often face an unexpected challenge when they sell to a corporate buyer or DSO that operates practices on an absentee basis. Having run many practices this way, Mike has experienced this firsthand.

Specifically, after training doctors to manage the practice well, there would come a time when he turned into a completely absentee owner—just like corporate buyers and DSOs. At first, that relationship would go well. With his efforts and expertise fresh in their minds, the doctors would have no qualms with sending him money: after all, he had helped them set things up and do a lot of work on the front-end.

Over time, however, the ongoing value he supplied to practices on a day-to-day basis started feeling arbitrary and disconnected from the money the doctors running the practice had to send him. The money wasn't worth their perception of the value he continued to bring, which put them at odds with one another.

Mike would end up selling those practices back to the doctors. Because he was able to structure his deal well, he could sell it at a price that was a good deal for them while providing himself with a 300% or 400% return on his investment, a healthy return for the value he provided.

At some point, any absentee owner is going to face grief from the doctors running their practices, so they have to be proactive about setting up their contract and picking the right kind of doctor. Mike picked doctors who could've gone out on their own and made it, and he just made it easier for them. That is exactly the kind of doctor who is going to chafe under the yoke of an absentee owner, longterm.

What the Dental Industry Will Look Like as the Window Closes

While the exact timeframe when the window of opportunity will close is uncertain, one thing is for sure: The practice of dentistry has already changed forever because of dental technology and insurance. When the dust settles, private practices will need to significantly adjust their models if they want to survive.

Mike expounds in detail:

"We have already been seeing the death of specialists and even boutique practices and a shift toward general practitioners who do everything in-house. We have seen it with cosmetic dentistry. It used to be a big pull to promote a general practice as being able to do cosmetic dentistry. Now, it's commonplace."

But Mike doesn't stop there.

"We have seen the same thing start with dental implants. At the beginning of the century, implant dentistry became big and few general dentists placed implants. Those who did were making big money. They were a more affordable alternative to specialists for patients but still a high-profit procedure for practices. Implants are still a great, high-profit service, but the market is getting saturated and competition for patients is stronger than ever."

"Eventually, all of these procedures will become commonplace and become necessary for survival, instead of a positive differentiator and profit booster. Small, independent practice ownership will become much more challenging."

I nod in agreement. If that proves true, practices will need to be open to multiple models and be even more intentional about matching their practice model with the demographics of their area. But Mike isn't finished.

"There always will be fee-for-service practices, but they aren't for every dentist. Institutions that teach boutique-style cosmetic dentistry are finding that people who take PPOs are offering the same services that boutique practices offer. Thus, those patients who want cosmetic services have no need to leave the doctor they trust to get procedures they want.

Although fee-for-service practices can work with the right demographic, doctors should seriously consider whether using PPO relationships might be necessary to continue attracting high-value procedures from the vast pool of patients insurance companies influence.

Additionally, you must understand the demographic of your location the patient pool that attracts and then match your model to the patient demographics in your area."

"What does that look like?"

"For example, I recently connected with a doctor who moved a cosmetic dentistry practice that had been doing well to a more affluent area. Almost immediately after opening the doors, he began to struggle. Eventually, he went bankrupt."

I lean in as Mike continues the story.

"The problem was, his cosmetic practice needed people with poor teeth to survive. But the people in a three-mile radius of his office all earned well over $100,000 per year. And the vast majority of those grew up in at least a middle-class family who brushed, flossed, and visited the dentist regularly. They probably didn't have problems that would need to be fixed by a cosmetic dentist. If they did, they caught it early and fixed it a long time ago."

I pause from my note-taking as Mike expounds further.

"Additionally, oral health has improved vastly over the past several decades. When I graduated in 1975, the average adult had about sixteen decayed, missing, or filled teeth. Today, the number is barely over three." His practice didn't fit the demographic of his new location, and he was competing against general practices that could perform cosmetic dentistry in-house for a shrinking pool of cosmetic patients."

He's right. Technology has changed ortho. It's changed endo. It's changed every aspect of dentistry. We even have at-home dentistry. Of course, most doctors know at-home dentistry isn't an adequate alternative for the quality of care you get from a dentist. However, many consumers are content with "good enough" care for many things, if it saves them money.

Taking Advantage of the Exit Window

When Mike graduated, the vast majority of doctors wanted to become owners soon after graduating. Today, less than half of doctors will become owners. That drop is a product of generational differences, economic factors, and more. Thus, even as more doctors are graduating, the pool of ready, willing, and able buyers is shrinking.

In Mike's experience, the majority of doctors just want to work for a company, earn a strong salary with good benefits and not have to worry about the responsibilities of practice ownership. That's really fueled corporations and DSOs in their ability to buy up practices. That's also driven up prices for strong practices higher than they have ever been.

"At some point, however, the pool of corporate and DSO buyers will run out," Mike warns.

I pause from my note-taking to ask a critical question rising in my mind. "What will cause the pool of corporate buyers and DSOs to quit buying? Are we just going to saturate the marketplace? How long will this window last?"

Mike's response hits hard.

"It's already happening. Corporate practices and DSOs are no longer the highest-growth sector of the dental industry. That honor has moved to multiple-doctor practices, which are growing at 20% per year, or more."

I can tell Mike is searching for an analogy to better illustrate his point.

"Take a look at the pharmacy industry. It took about eighteen years for giants like CVS to realize the value of them buying small pharmacies had run its course. In essence, they started thinking, 'Why would we want to buy a mom-and-pop business with no retail sales and crappy systems when we can just do our own big box stores?'

My mind races back to my previous interviews with Brady and Dustin -- they affirmed this exact same point.

"Medicine was the same way. Hospitals used to be not-for-profit. Today, they are all for-profit. A DSO or large corporation is very similar to how hospitals run, today. They control the market and determine what doctors can practice where. If you don't have privileges at a hospital, you can't practice there. And if you're not associated with a hospital, your patient pool shrinks dramatically. Doctors' pay has also dropped significantly during that transition."

"With dentistry, unless something changes dramatically, we might have ten years left before the window closes and corporations turn their attention away from dentistry and DSOs move to almost exclusively opening their own practices."

Mike warns, however, that planning your sale is not *just* about planning the sale. You *must* also be prepared for what comes after the sale. Because this is so important, it's a big part of what I help doctors do with Freedom Founders.

How does this play out? Here's an email a doctor sent to Mike:

> *Dr. Abernathy,*
>
> *A few years ago, I came away from a dental conference about retirement convinced that my planning was sufficient, my associate was doing well,*

and that I'd get a relatively good price to
sell my business.

I liked your words and thinking. I had a
great relationship with a potential buyer,
the sale went through very well for me,
holding an employment contract for two
years with the new buyer. But at the end
of two years I was let go.

This happens all the time, and neither Mike nor I are surprised. It's incredibly difficult to change roles at a practice. If you sell to a corporate buyer or DSO, you can get top dollar and a salary to stay on, but your role will change significantly. You will have the benefit of fewer responsibilities, but you will also have the *burden* of less authority and autonomy. That's why it's so important to not only prepare *your practice* for sale but also prepare *yourself* for the next season of life, if you want to take advantage of this unique transition window.

How does Mike counsel doctors he helps navigate transition?

"I tell doctors who want to stay on, 'Yeah, in about six weeks, they're going to hate you.' This doctor who emailed me had a written contract for two years employment with a 'gentleman's agreement' that he could continue for as long as he wanted. When he was let go, he was subject to a two-year non-compete and only had $1,000,000 in retirement. He needed to work and was stuck in a changing dental marketplace in North Carolina, a state with a big corporate dentistry presence."

I grimace at the thought, before offering my next question. "What do you hope every doctor knew about transition that's not being talked about enough? What can doctors do to avoid getting in a similar situation to the doctor who emailed you?"

Dr. Abernathy doesn't hesitate a bit before responding confidently:

"You need to start preparing three or five years ahead of time. Really bring up the value of your practice so that it's appealing to more buyers. Do the best you can and make sure to take care of yourself. Prepare for what happens after the transaction closes, which is often the biggest adjustment doctors face no matter what method of exit they move forward with. Finally, be open to alternative ways to exit, such as through fractional shares."

There it is, again. Another expert targeting three to five years to prepare a practice for sale, which puts us square in the middle of this unique window of opportunity to sell before the big money disappears. And with decades of experience consulting for doctors, pay close attention to Mike's emphasis on preparing for what comes next.

Takeaways

- With corporations and DSOs focusing on buying through acquisition, the pool of individual buyers is diminishing. The most common sale of a practice is to another doctor, although that is typically for practices selling in the $650,000 range. If your practice has grown beyond that, corporate buyers, DSOs, or even fractional sales might be worth considering to maximize your return.

- Many corporate buyers are dentists turned entrepreneurs who have created systems and processes that allow practices to run efficiently with three or more locations. If you want to transition into entrepreneurship, adjusting your systems to work without needing your energy and charisma is critical. What happens with your second location will be critical. If you can get past two, your upside is unlimited.

- DSOs and corporate buyers are appealing for someone who just wants to do dentistry and not deal with the hassle of running a business. But the benefits of not running a business must be weighed against the burden of having less authority and autonomy.

- If you own multiple practices, a transaction with a DSO or corporate buyer could be smoother for you in the long term because you and your team will be more accustomed to shared responsibilities.

- Selling a fractional share of your practice can help maximize your return if your practice is too big for a single dentist to purchase and a corporate buyer or DSO transaction isn't a good fit. But it can take more time and will require you to continue in your role of leadership and management as you navigate the sale.

- Technology, insurance, and the attention of corporate buyers and DSOs will forever change dentistry. In the next five to ten years, succeeding as a small, independent practice will become much more difficult. You will need to perform high-value procedures to stay relevant and match your practice structure with the pool of patients in your area.

- Preparing for your exit is not just about your practice. It's also about your person. You must prepare for the next season of your life to avoid finding yourself still needing income from practicing dentistry beyond any guaranteed contractual transition period.

To listen to the audio recording of my interview with Dr. Mike Abernathy, go to:

www.SellingYourPracticeBook.com/Interviews

Chapter 5 - Dr. Paul Goodman

Due Diligence and the Future of Private Practice

Dr. Paul "Nacho" Goodman has been practicing dentistry for more than a decade, running a growing multi-location practice in New Jersey with an active residency program. He is one of the most engaged professionals in the dental industry: He has purchased three dental practices with his brother, he has built several on-demand courses to help dentists run and grow their own practices, and he consults for doctors looking to do the same. He also acts as a dental practice broker, helping buyers and sellers navigate practice sales, and working with doctors and team members to manage patient expectations during transitions. He has packed the equivalent of several decades of experience into slightly more than one.

With such broad experience, Paul has a unique perspective on exit strategies. So I decided to give him a call and get his insights.

Paul kicks off our conversation by talking about how he's seeing the buyer mix evolving and where he expects it to go over the next five to ten years. Like the other experts, Paul sees corporate buyers and DSOs growing their influence with solo doctors reducing theirs:

"The people who could buy a practice in the "olden days" were just people who looked like the selling dentist but younger. Buyers used to be younger dentists looking to take over from older dentists."

This reminds me of Brady's comments on the changing values of today's millennial dentists, which leads me to ask: "As corporate buyers and DSOs buy up more practices, how can solo doctors best position themselves?"

Paul leads on confidently.

"One way to compete against corporate practices and DSOs is to collaborate with other doctors to build a bigger business strategy around dentistry."

I wonder what that might look like, but Paul is eager to elaborate. "For example, while younger doctors are still the biggest group of buyers, their relative inexperience often makes them want a seller to stick around for longer than a group of experienced general practice doctors would need. Additionally, younger solo doctors often have financial constraints that experienced doctors do not. Creative collaborations, thus, put entrepreneurial doctors at an advantage over younger solo-doctor buyers."

"Additionally, while small groups don't have as much funding as larger corporate practices, they often have enough money to compete on individual practices. The small group nature also gives doctor groups more flexibility to negotiate purchase terms that would not fit the model of a more structured corporate or DSO practice."

Paul and his brother use the flexibility, experience, and the relationships they build through their residency program to find practices that are attractive to them but would not fit the DSO model. Specifically, if doctors just want to sell and retire, DSOs tend to not be interested in buying their practices because their model generally calls for the seller to stick around for three or four years. Paul and his brother, on the other hand, can pull from their practice and residency program and don't need the same commitment to make a practice purchase attractive.

But what if someone doesn't want to grow? What if they are ready to get out of dentistry in three to five years? What should they do?

I ask Paul these questions.

"This happens all the time. If you're not looking to grow and compete against big dental groups as the market change, you do have options. You could spend a few years growing and then sell the bigger practice. Or, you could spend some time preparing your practice to sell and stay on for at least some period of time to make a smooth transition."

Paul continued.

"But some dentists wait too long to sell their practice, become emotionally drained, and just sort of say, 'I'm ready to go now!' They call me to broker a sale, and I have to break the news to them that a quick sale is not something that's very common. As the broker, I often tell them it might be twelve to eighteen months before they're allowed to go."

"If they're nearing retirement age and want to be done quicker, a younger associate looking to purchase their first practice might be a good fit. But they won't maximize their return. If they can wait a few years before exiting their practice, they could see a higher return by selling to a corporate buyer or DSO."

"So who are these groups?" I ask. "Where are they coming from?"

"Right now there are more and more groups that are coming into the market, ones I've never even heard of," Paul admits. "I'll list a practice for sale and get inquiries from groups I never even knew existed. That's a good thing for sellers while that window is open because those buyers have a variety of structures, business goals, and requirements. Right now, there is a bigger pool of buyers today than I've ever seen before."

"Interesting," I think to myself, then ask, "If a practice owner is prepared to do what it takes to sell to a corporate buyer or DSO, what do you think they should know?"

Paul speaks from experience as he elaborates:

"A lot of dentists show me contract proposals from a DSO that wants to buy their practice, but it's more of a consulting offer. The writing says the DSO is going to be a consultant, and if the numbers and stars align then they'll buy the practice at eight times EBITDA. I see it as a lot of big promises from companies that aren't really interested in the buyout but are instead looking for a consulting gig."

"Years ago, a dentist would sell their practice to somebody who wants to work it for thirty years and live a life like they had. Today, that's rarely the case, especially when selling to corporate buyers or DSOs. These groups could be in and out of a practice in two or three years, signing what essentially amounts to consulting agreements with practices and then selling out to an even bigger player. In their world, that's normal. That's their model. Buy control of a bunch of smaller practices, work with them for a short time, and then sell for a higher multiple to a bigger group."

My own experience confirms this picture. Selling your practice to a DSO might seem too good to be true—you get to exit in a few years and sell your practice for what it's worth—and, often, it is too good to be true. As Paul's grandmother once told him, "There's no such thing as a free nacho lunch."

It sounds to me that there's more to DSOs than the high prices they typically pay when they find the right practice.

Paul agrees that these buyers are more sophisticated than people think and often structure lopsided deals when they sense a practice owner is not very business savvy. This often happens by offering a higher purchase price than solo-doctor buyers but with caveats that make the deal much worse than meets the eye.

"The devil is in the details, and they are often a lot savvier business negotiators than most doctors. So, while practice owners can get a sweetheart deal from corporate buyers or DSOs, it's critical to have a really good team of professionals on your side."

Paul's voice becomes stronger with conviction.

"Unless a dentist has a really good attorney on their side, they're going to get taken advantage of. They're going to get beat by someone who's better at the dental business than them. When a dentist decides to sell their million-dollar-plus, five-operatory practice, they get overwhelmed with the number of buyers."

I nod as Paul continues.

"A good, dentist-focused attorney knows how to put together a transaction just like the doctors they represent know how to put in a veneer. These big groups have teams of attorneys. They're in it for themselves. So they make asset purchase agreements that are in their favor. It's up to the dentist to push back, do research, get their own team, and ask questions. The sale of their practice is often the biggest decision of their life, and it can easily be a bad decision if they underestimate the intentions of a DSO that wants to buy their practice."

I agree vigorously. In Freedom Founders, we call this type of preparation and homework "due diligence." Paul's words are definitely ringing true.

"Sometimes, the way a DSO deal is structured only seems like a higher price than selling to a solo dentist on paper. But in reality, the seller is unlikely to receive the entire purchase price. For example, if a practice is selling for $800,000, a solo doctor might take out a loan for the purchase price plus some working capital, less the down payment. At closing, the seller gets the entire final purchase price.

A DSO often has the money available and won't need to borrow. And they might offer the seller $1 million for the same practice. But instead of the seller getting the full sales price at closing, they might give $750,000 at closing and tie the additional $250,000 to post-closing performance."

I scan my notes, doing the math. Paul's example seems to make sense. While the higher purchase price looks good on paper, practice owners frequently never get a penny of the post-closing dollars. Sometimes, the performance goals are unattainable. Other times, the DSO shuts down the practice after running it for a while, deciding it was not worth their time. With large portfolios of practices, shutting one down is a much easier decision than it would be for a solo doctor. Still other times, the DSO itself is poorly run and goes out of business.

Paul's point is clear: before moving forward with a sales transaction, you must vet the buyer just like they vet you. A good broker can help you do that. They know buyers and can spot the warning signs. They know what questions to ask and can even bring multiple buyers to the table, competing against each other, thus giving the buyer more leverage to negotiate a good deal.

The Future of Corporate Buyers and DSOs

While Paul echoes what the other experts are saying about the retirement window closing, he adds a level of nuance through his insights into how the timeframe could vary based on your location:

"In dense areas and popular areas to live in, corporate buyers and DSOs will likely be buying existing practices longer than in less competitive areas. In demographically favorable areas like Center City, Philadelphia, or Dallas, startups require a lot of work, and many DSOs aren't willing to do the work it takes to make one successful. That's not their model. They could likely buy five existing practices with the same effort it would take to build one startup in those areas. They want to buy existing practices with a strong patient base. And they have plenty of practices to purchase in those areas."

Paul continues:

"In less competitive areas, however, corporate buyers and DSOs will likely shift toward building startups sooner rather than later. Not only are there fewer practices available for purchase in those areas, it does not take a lot of work to launch a successful startup. This is similar to what happened with pharmacy and medicine, launching startup facilities in less competitive areas while focusing on acquisitions for a longer period of time in more competitive areas."

Alternatives to DSOs and Sales to Other Doctors

What about the fractional sale? Is that a viable model for doctors looking to exit over the next several years? Paul doesn't think so, except in rare circumstances:

"Fewer and fewer of fractional sales are working out these days. Outside of two circumstances, we rarely see fractional sales work out well as an exit plan. The first circumstance is with a family relationship. The second is with an associate whose spouse is independently successful and can support a long-term path to practice ownership."

Paul then thoughtfully adds,

"If you can navigate this type of transaction, they can end up outstanding because the buyer has an experienced dentist helping them. The problem is most younger dentists don't have the ability to be financially patient, funding the purchase of a fractional interest. If they borrow from a bank, a large portion of their salary and distribution will go to paying down the debt. The same is true if the practice finances the purchase. Usually the owner can't give enough to their associates to compete with a corporate starting salary. It has to be a long-term plan with the associate willing to take home less than they could in a corporate practice to earn equity and higher revenue years in the future. With student debt and other financial demands on younger dentists these days, it usually takes an associate with a successful spouse who can take care of their bills while the bulk of the associate's salary goes toward buying shares in the practice."

The Future Landscape for Independent Practices

We continued to discuss how the landscape for independent practices will be dramatically different in a few years or so. Solo dentists will have a difficult time competing against group practices unless they rise to the top of the industry to attract and retain patients who care more about having *them* as their dentist than the cost savings they can often achieve through group practices. To occupy this elite position, a dentist will need superior clinical, personality, and communication skills. Because it will take a lot of work, this path is only for doctors who have a true passion for building a top practice. One more caveat: you need to have the right location for the practice to make sure you have enough patients to sustain your top-tier practice.

An easier path to success will be for doctors to create their own group practices -- the model Paul and his brother have chosen.

Paul likens this approach to the restaurant industry. Running a high-end restaurant takes a lot of work and attention to detail. Not all chefs have the talent and passion to thrive, and not all areas will have favorable demographics. Despite the odds, a few become "Top Chefs" who attract a consistent flow of customers willing to pay a big premium for the exclusive food and experience. Like "Top Chef" restaurants, concierge or boutique dental practices take a lot of work. It's an exhausting, risky venture.

Paul recalls watching an interview of Top Chef, Nicolas Elmi, of the renowned Philadelphia restaurant, Laurel. Complimenting Laurel, the interviewer asked Elmi if he planned to open another. Elmi almost spit out his water before responding passionately, "God, no! Do you have any idea? I want to see my kids!"

"Chefs and dentists are so alike," Paul explains. "They want to open up quick service food like Taco Bell. When you go to Taco Bell, you know what you're getting. Nobody pretends it's gourmet food. but Taco Bell still has plenty of business. A Taco Bell dental practice would get plenty of business, too. And it would be much less risky for dentists moving forward if they can grow their group enough to leverage economies of scale."

I know many of my colleagues would cringe at that remark. But it does ring true -- Paul has a lot of business savvy.

"One way to achieve economies of scale without growing too big of a group practice is to collaborate with other dentists in your area as much as possible. For example, you could consider associate sharing with other practices. You can get the dentists in your town together, figure out how many days a week each dentist needs an associate, what days they need that associate, and get that associate a schedule to help everyone out at their practice.

Another option is to build a building with other dentists. Most of the time, the buildings that dental offices are built in aren't great. They're usually just little condos. Two dentists could build a building together with ten operatories and give each other room to grow and the flexibility to collaborate in other ways. That flexibility can help even beat a DSO if the dentists collaborate well.

Collaborative ventures will also put dentists in a better position to compete against another tough adversary: insurance companies. Solo practices have very little leverage to negotiate favorable deals, whereas group practices with higher volume will be able to negotiate much better rates.

As strange as it might sound, the biggest obstacle and challenge dentists will have is not making group practices work from an operations perspective, but from a conflict management perspective. With a solo practice, a dentist runs the whole show with their systems and processes, but that will not be a sustainable model anymore. As they grow and collaborate, they will need to manage multiple conflicts with multiple doctors and teams used to different systems."

I lean back in my chair. This is a lot to take in. My mind races to summarize...

If you're near retirement or like the idea of exiting in the next three to five years, you can insulate yourself from the hard work it will take to survive in the future. Get a trusted team together to prepare and market your practice for sale. Over the next few years, you will likely be able to get out on your own timeline with a healthy sales price.

But if you are more than five to ten years away from wanting to exit your practice, you will need to get creative to survive the toughening market. Corporate and DSO practices will make it incredibly difficult to compete if you want to stay independent and continue to practice.

Takeaways

- The buyer mix is becoming increasingly diverse, and new DSOs and corporate buyers are flooding the market. With increased options, however, it becomes all the more important to vet buyers to make sure they don't have weak finances or a habit of closing down practices they purchase.

- The best way to get top dollar for your practice is to have an experienced broker market your practice for sale. Not only can they attract multiple buyers for a strong practice but they can help vet buyers to help you protect yourself.

- While DSOs and corporate buyers will continue buying practices in highly competitive areas for a longer period of time, they will likely shift to building startup practices in less competitive areas sooner.

- Fractional shares can work well but generally only with family transfers or with an associate who can afford to earn a lower income than they could get in other practices while they pay down their buy-in.

- Solo practices will struggle to compete against group, corporate, and DSO practices moving forward, except for rare dentists with the talent and passion to become the equivalent of a "Top Chef" in dentistry.

- Independent group practices can still thrive in the future, especially if they collaborate and manage conflict well.

To listen to the audio recording of my interview with Dr. Paul Goodman, go to:

www.SellingYourPracticeBook.com/Interviews

Chapter 6 - Timothy Lott, CPA

Financing, Changing Demographics, and Future Trends

Tim Lott is a CPA and certified valuation analyst who provides consulting services to dental professionals and practices. He consults on all aspects of practice purchase, sale, and structure, including associate, partner, and shareholder arrangements; practice management and purchase; sales, buy-ins and buy-outs and the related tax issues.

His vast experience navigating practice transactions gives him a unique perspective on how the market has evolved and what it will look like in the future. So, who does he see as the most active buyers in the current market?

> *"The vast majority of buyers are still doctors who have been out of school for three to five years and are looking to become owners."*

This observation resonates with Dr. Abernathy's perspective. Even with so much money flowing from corporate buyers and DSOs, it does not seem to be taking away from solo dentists, at least in the short term.

I wonder whether there are any philosophical differences between these new doctors and past generations. Obviously, it's dangerous to over-generalize an entire generation, but millennials tend to have different priorities. For example, one common trait that has been observed with millennials is the commitment to achieving more balance in their lives. Whereas older generations may have *desired* more balance, millennials appear to be more willing to sacrifice things like money or prestige to enjoy a better work-life balance.

In Tim's experience, he finds that, while some millennials learn that practice ownership isn't a good fit for them, there are plenty looking to become owners.

"I coach a lot of millennial buyers about the reality of practice ownership even before they get to the point of looking at a practice. Obviously, practice ownership is a lot of work. There are things you can do to make it easier, and I talk with all first-time buyers about what it takes to be successful as a practice owner to ascertain whether they are prepared to get into running a business, not just millennials. Sometimes, they come to realize that practice ownership might not be a good fit for them, for sure. But many of them do move forward and have become very successful owners."

That said, buying a practice three to five years out of school while hundreds of thousands of dollars in debt seems risky. Yet, that demographic still represents the vast majority of buyers of practices, even if some of the prices are inflated.

So, I ask Tim whether their debt load slows them down.

"It doesn't seem to shrink the pool much at all. In fact, the same dentists who carry $300,000, $400,000, or even $500,000 in debt quickly come to understand it will take a long time to pay off their student loans if they stick to being associates. They realize practice ownership is really the quickest way out of debt, even if it requires them to go into additional debt to purchase a practice."

That makes sense. It also makes sense that doctors who went hundreds of thousands of dollars into debt for dental school would be more inclined to go into additional debt to finance a practice. They obviously see the benefit of financing a better financial future, so the biggest barrier might be finding a lender, rather than getting comfortable with additional debt.

With hundreds of thousands of dollars of debt, is it difficult for this group of buyers to finance a transaction? Do they take longer than selling to a DSO or other, more financially secure buyer?

"Ten plus years ago, it was much more difficult than it is today. It used to be that banks wouldn't lend a lot of money to a buyer with less than five years' experience and a mountain of student debt. Since then, however, new lenders have entered the market. Some of those lenders have been very aggressive, too. They have loaned higher amounts and helped finance purchases for doctors with less than five years' experience and a lot of student debt."

"With banks aggressively entering the market to fund dental practice transactions, traditional lenders have been forced to become more aggressive themselves, even lending to buyers with much higher student debt than in the past. But the value of the practice has to justify the additional borrowing. It used to be that a bank could cap their financing at one million dollars on the larger practices and force the seller to lend the difference in the purchase price."

"Today, if the value is there and the practice has an associate or two staying on, it's possible to get most of the financing from the lenders these days without the seller lending any of the price. I even helped a solo buyer get $2.8 million from a bank to buy a practice doing about $3.5 million in revenue. This buyer had good experience and the seller was willing to stick around for a couple of years. That helped. But more and more lenders are willing to lend $1.5 million, $2 million, and sometimes more, if the transaction justifies it."

As a CPA, Tim's perspective on financing transactions is noteworthy. For example, one thing Tim also mentions is that sometimes doctors are too conservative with the practices they target, especially those doctors who are willing and able to produce at a high level themselves. If they're capable of producing $600,000, $700,000, $800,000, or $900,000, their production justifies buying a practice in the $1 million or $1.2 million range. Many times, those doctors end up buying a practice for $600,000 and below and have a harder time maximizing the practice value.

These two factors—the more aggressive lending environment for doctors plus Tim's suggestion that some doctors might be better served buying a bigger practice than they otherwise would—suggest doctors looking to exit during this window of inflated practice prices have more options to maximize their practice value than selling to a corporate buyer or DSO. Specifically, if your practice falls into this low-seven-figure range and you do not want the post-closing responsibilities that go along with corporate and DSO sales, you might find a hardworking doctor willing to work with an aggressive lender to buy you out.

Aside from post-closing opportunities, what are the downsides of selling to a DSO if you want to keep all your options open? Some make pretty hefty promises to practice owners. Do they follow through? Have any of Tim's clients regretted selling to a DSO?

"It depends on the seller. When the DSOs are buying practices, there's typically an additional earn-out or a contractual lock-up. But they want to keep the doctor in place for two, three, or maybe up to five years. It depends on the individual doctor—how resilient they are, how willing they are to adapt to a new culture and takeover."

"If they're a seller in their mid-to-late sixties and ready to retire, semi-retire, or scale back, the DSO model can work well. If they're a younger seller, meaning in their forties or fifties, and are ready to move onto something else, they're probably willing to work for less because they got their payment on their practice up front. For those types of doctors, young and old, they're willing to scale back and gradually retire despite getting less pay."

"If they're at the point in life where they want out, then and there, and they aren't okay with staying on for a while and being paid less for their work than they were as the practice owner, a DSO model isn't going to work for them. It's really driven by the type of seller they are. I have seen a lot of those sellers who are in their forties or early fifties who really do want to work clinically, but they're ready cash in their ownership chips. They know they'll be getting paid a little less than what they're pulling down from their practice, but that's okay with them. They know if they get the itch to rebuild something, they can move to a different state or a different county and do it all over again."

"The clients I've worked with are glad they did it, but we made sure it was a good fit for them before they moved forward."

So, in Tim's experience, younger dentists tend to be more aggressive when it comes to borrowing. And banks have become more aggressive when it comes to lending. That opened up a whole new pool of buyers for practices.

At the same time, we frequently hear that people are not retiring like they used to. They retire later in life. When they retire, they also don't quit cold turkey, hand in their keys and leave with a gold watch. Many people across industries phase themselves out of work. How does that impact the market? Are fewer practices being sold because older doctors are hanging on longer?

"There are certainly a lot more dentists semi-retiring today than there were years ago, but that doesn't necessarily mean they are not selling their practices. They have other options. Those older doctors might be more interested in selling to a DSO and staying on for two to five years. Or, they might be interested in selling fractional shares, although that has become much harder to do than years ago."

So, is fractional ownership gaining momentum with this older group of doctors staying on longer? How does that compare with selling to one doctor or a corporate or PPO buyer?

"As much as doctors are doing more phaseouts than cold turkey retirements, fractional ownership isn't very popular these days. Back in the 1980s, it was the primary model. When someone wanted to retire in five years, they'd find an associate, have them work one, two, or three days a week, and then add more as the doctor cut back until they took over the practice."

"Today, because there are so many more buyers, sellers are less likely to go down that road of hiring an associate and dealing with the management of that associate issue for so many years. They'd rather work for another three, four, or five years, maximize profitability, and then execute on an exit plan and move onto the next phase of their life.

"Nowadays," Tim says, "when somebody's ready to sell the practice, they're ready to sell 100% of it."

"I just don't see fractional practice sales much, outside of larger multi-doctor, multi-owner type practices elevating associates to partner. In those cases, you might have a fractional owner want to retire and an associate take over their shares. Not only do the practice owners have options, the associates do too. It's getting harder and harder to find an associate to take over on a fractional basis. With so many other types of buyers, it's just not a good fit for most practices."

Signs the Window is Closing

As a CPA and valuation expert, Tim has deep insights into what's been driving the rise in practice values. Thus, he is also uniquely positioned to look for warning signs that the window is closing. I ask him how we might be able to spot the market slowing down.

"The fact is, we have very low interest rates today—historically low. They look to remain low over the next few years. That helps. If they rise, the cost to service practice debt will be higher, obviously. That could certainly impact the amount doctors are able to borrow. Additionally, if we end up in a recession where credit constricts again across the board, that would impact dental lending as well."

"Moreover, if banks go back to being more conservative, doctors might not be able to finance higher-value practices, reducing the buyer pool. That could impact practice value as well as the ability of a doctor to exit quickly or without the post-closing responsibilities corporate buyers or DSOs typically ask for."

"DSOs and corporate buyers could also get to a point where they're not as interested in buying existing practices and focus on growing through startups.

If all these things happen at once, it's certainly possible that prices and transaction volume could fall quickly, although we typically do have at least some warning."

He also noted that it's possible for government regulations to negatively impact the dental market or the corporate and DSOs practice model in general. Those phenomena are hard to predict but certainly can happen.

Tim didn't come across as signaling a precipitous drop anytime in the next few years. That said, it is certainly possible to see interest rates creep up, the economy slow down, and corporate buyers and DSOs adjusting their model over the course of two or three years. And healthcare reform is definitely a major focus in state and federal politics.

Thus, if your plan is to eventually exit the practice and move into a new phase of your life, and it takes two or three years to prepare your practice for sale, it would definitely be wise to start preparing. After all, cleaning up finances and operations can benefit you as an owner even if you decide not to sell in the next few years, so there doesn't seem to be much downside to being prepared.

So, if a practice owner wants to take advantage of this window, I ask Tim what he suggests they do to maximize their practice value, outside of cleaning up their financials and operations. His response is thoughtful.

"If you can reduce the number of PPOs you participate with, stick with the ones with the highest reimbursements and do more fee-for-service work, you can make your practice much more profitable and attractive in just a few years."

"When my clients do this, one of two things happens almost every time. Most of the time their profitability goes up significantly, assuming they're doing all the other things right. It's about keeping the higher reimbursement PPOs and dropping the lower ones, even if they're seeing fewer patients."

"Other times, they make the same amount of money but see fewer patients. Many have been able to make the same money and cut back half a day a week. So, those gain because they get a better quality of life for the same money. That's just like making more money—your life is fuller, your life is richer, and sometimes that's what it's all about. Sometimes, it's better. And to a buyer, a practice making the same money in less time is worth more. So, either way, your practice value goes up."

Takeaways

- The vast majority of buyers remain solo doctors a few years out of school.

- With lenders more willing to finance practice purchasers, younger doctors are able to borrow more money than they used to. That means they can buy healthy practices for $1.5 million, $2 million, or more, even if they still have hundreds of thousands of dollars in student debt.

- A DSO is good to sell to if you're looking to scale back, and you don't mind getting paid a little less for a few years. Of those practice owners Tim has helped sell to DSOs, Tim has never met one who regrets it.

- Fractional sales used to be popular but are very hard to make work these days, given the number of options for both practice owners and associates.

- In the last five to ten years, DSO's have increased the buyer pool and increased demand, which has raised practice values. But if DSOs move on, start opening more of their own practices, or have to change their current model due to government regulation, values will go down.

- If you are looking to maximize your practice value, don't limit your focus to cleaning up your finances and organization. Take a look at your insurance mix, too. Maintain relationships with the two or three providers that have the highest reimbursements and do fee-for-service with the rest. This allows you to increase profits or reduce the time you need to work for the money you're currently making. Either way, your practice value goes up.

To listen to the audio recording of my interview with Tim Lott, go to:

www.SellingYourPracticeBook.com/Interviews

Chapter 7 - Jerry Jones

Entrepreneurial Leadership in the Face of Transition

Jerry Jones is a good friend of mine. We share the "entrepreneurial bug." He brings a unique perspective to owning, operating, and transitioning out of the practice of dentistry. He is not a dentist but an entrepreneur who has bought, sold, or started twenty businesses, including several dental practices. Taking advantage of the current market for dental practices, Jerry sold his last practice in May 2018 and moved deeper into his other business ventures.

Jerry's broad business background is impressive. Dentists don't tend to be entrepreneurial by nature, even if many of us do end up owning a practice. We don't tend to be great at buying, selling, or starting multiple businesses. We typically get into a practice and run it until we are ready to find our next. Yet Jerry has been owned *eighteen* businesses, including more dental practices than most dentists own in their careers.

As a non-dentist who has bought and sold a number of dental practices, Jerry brings a valuable perspective. So, I wanted to talk with him about the state of the dental industry, why he got in, why he got out when he did, and what he learned that can help doctors during this unique retirement window.

The first thing I ask Jerry about is a bit of his business background and how it led him to own dental practices. He responds thoughtfully, his eyes wandering about the room as he recalls scenes from his childhood.

"I caught the entrepreneurial bug from twelve years old when I made a deal with my neighbor to mow her lawn ten times in exchange for her little riding lawn mower." He smiles sheepishly as the memory came to life on the movie screen of his mind, "It had a 10-horsepower Tecumsah engine and I wasn't happy about that. I wanted a Briggs and Stratton."

I laugh as he continues.

"I used that junky old Tecumsah to mow more lawns and saved enough to upgrade my equipment, buying a better mower and weed eater. Before long, I had five accounts in the neighborhood and was busy in the summertimes.

That's when I realized -- it doesn't take capital to make money, it takes creative thinking."

I nod vigorously. My own childhood business ventures come to mind as Jerry continues.

"That entrepreneurial spirit followed me into adulthood. My first significant company was a credit reporting business, conducting tenant screening for landlords. A short while—and additional businesses later—I started working for a dentist named Travis McFee. Travis was, and still is, an entrepreneurial guy."

"One of the businesses Travis owned shipped magazines, envelopes, and letterhead to dentists for them to send to their patients. All the dentists needed to do was run the letterhead through their copy machines, stuff it with the magazines into an envelope, and mail it to their patients. Eventually, I bought that business from Travis and grew it. Pretty soon I was doing direct mail postcards, internet marketing for dentists, and more."

"The more I learned about dental practices, the more they intrigued me as an entrepreneur. So, I decided to look into practice ownership."

I can't help but laugh. Jerry joins me, good naturedly. "I'm kind of a sucker for fun," he states, smiling, before continuing.

"The law at the time didn't allow me to buy a practice or own charts. But it allowed me to start a practice and 'hire' a dentist who owned the charts, so I found a dentist and built a business around that doctor, who maintained ownership of the charts. Pretty soon thereafter, I added another doctor, and another doctor, and another. At one point, I had four doctors working at the same time."

I raise my hand for a question.

"These doctors were all associates? They didn't have any financial interest in the actual practice?"

"Right. Yes." Jerry nods. "Every time a patient was generated from marketing efforts and they were booked with a doctor, that doctor then owned that chart as long as they were with the practice. If they left, we structured it so another dentist took over ownership of those charts."

I love Jerry's story - he is a true entrepreneur. I wanted to dig deeper and learn more. "So what did you have to learn in order to make this work?"

"I didn't find it very different, to be honest. Every business has its unique issues. Dentistry had different services and revenue structures than other business, but at the end of the day, business is business. Dentistry was just a new model. I didn't even know what a crown was when I opened my dental office. I didn't know what a root canal was. I couldn't read an x-ray, and still can't. I learned a little bit about dentistry, so I could understand my business. But I only needed to learn just enough. I hired doctors to take care of the clinical stuff."

Spoken like a true business leader and entrepreneur. Jerry is clearly a business expert. He continued.

"The clinical practice of dentistry was 100% under the auspices of the Oregon Dental Board, which helped. Basically, if you practiced dentistry, you had to do what the board told you to do. Because I wasn't practicing dentistry, I made it clear to everyone that they needed to do what was right for their role. I told them, specifically, 'I don't want to know anything about clinical because clinical is not the business that I'm in. I'm in the business of attracting and retaining customers. I'm in the marketing business. Your job and your role here is to treat the patient the best way you can possibly treat them. And I'm going to stay out of your way. I don't want to talk about anything clinical, but my job is to present patients to you and help you keep them within the confines of your practice, the charts.'"

I nod. Those conversations can be powerful in business because they define each person's role and set expectations. It let everyone know the value they were receiving from each other, thus making it much easier for Jerry to operate on an absentee basis without creating conflict with the doctors.

Jerry continued by sharing that one of the first things he learned when he opened his practice was that, out of necessity, doing dentistry ties dentists to chairs. They can't get away from doing the clinical side of things, so they can't be absentee owners unless they divorce themselves from doing dentistry. They can't escape the office if they're tied to the chair. As a non-dentist owner, he had a distinct advantage in that regard. As a practitioner and owner during my own career, I certainly experienced this firsthand.

"The advantage was that I could talk to patients about how they were treated as a human in my practice instead of being busy moving to the next patient like most dentist/owners are. It allowed me the freedom to continue to operate my marketing company while having a dental office at the same time. The disadvantage was that I couldn't do the dentistry and couldn't talk to a patient about the dental care. So, I could not have as in-depth conversations with them about the clinical side of things."

Jerry's success on an absentee basis is unique. But I wonder whether he hit some bumps in the road. Sure enough, he did.

For Jerry, it just seemed to him that if he wasn't in the office, things would not run as smoothly because nobody had ownership of the operations. A strong office manager or chief of operations who has a great deal of latitude could have helped, but nothing beats an on-site owner, in Jerry's experience. Thus, if you're looking to transition out, in order to start a new phase of life, it might not be wise to try to structure things to make you an absentee owner. Not only will you miss out on the cash infusion received from a sale, but you will likely find your business run inefficiently and feel the need to be there more frequently than you would like.

Jerry didn't want to be onsite, so he hired a top-flight chief of operations to run the business. One observation Jerry had about non-doctor ownership is that it tends to create confusion, especially among the DAs, hygienists, and other staff members. Even though Jerry signed their checks, they worked all day with the doctors and would listen to their instructions over Jerry's. The chief of operations helped but eventually, Jerry decided it was time to take advantage of an inflated market, cash out, and move onto his next season of life.

Jerry's experience highlights several important points about getting involved with corporate owners and DSOs. In Jerry's case, the law required him to start a practice from scratch. That means there were not years— sometimes *decades*—of standard operating procedures in place, or a senior dentist on staff who had been running the place for ages. Despite being able to start fresh, Jerry still experienced operational challenges when it came to managing the team as an absentee owner. If a corporate buyer or DSO buys an existing practice and wants to institute its own policies and procedures, the likelihood for conflict is even higher. It's important to be prepared for that, especially because you'd typically need to stay on for a couple of years post-closing.

One lesson Jerry learned in business is the importance of clearly outlining an exit strategy for each business he would open or buy. He'd have it outlined well in advance of even taking the first steps, a strategy that set him apart from the average dentist. In fact, the more he learned about the dental market, the more he realized many dentists don't think about their exits. They think about opening, running, sometimes growing, but rarely exit strategies. This is a costly mistake. As he elaborated:

"Knowing an exit strategy in advance is absolutely key because you just don't know when it's time to leave or when you should leave. You don't know when you've got what you wanted out of it. For most dentists, the first business they sell is their practice towards the end of their career, and they hesitate to exit at a young age even if their hearts are no longer in dentistry."

"That's very true," I think to myself. Doing *anything* for the first time can be daunting. Much more so if it is a seven-figure transaction that involves your life work.

Sunk Cost Fallacy

"The problem is that they often struggle with sunk cost fallacy," Jerry states. "They've gone to school, gotten years of education, come out with massive amounts of debt, and they start up or buy a practice. They are hundreds of thousands, if not more than a million dollars and a decade plus into their dental career."

"Over time, they know inside they lost the spark—or never had it to begin with. But they invested so much time and money into dentistry, they stick with it, even if it makes them miserable, to get a return on their time and money."

"Sunk cost fallacy. That's a big one." I think to myself, recalling recent blog posts I've written on the subject.

"The sunk cost fallacy leads to a lot of identity issues. Many professionals struggle with this. They can't separate themselves as a human from themselves as a professional. For example, if someone asked five dental colleagues, "Tell me about yourself?" what do you think they would say? Typically, the first thing out of their mouths is, 'I'm a dentist,' not a mother, father, husband, wife, athlete, art collector, real estate investor, or any other number of things that really make them an interesting person. Their first response when people ask them to state their identity is their profession."

Jerry continues.

"Sometimes it's hard to separate your identity from your profession before you visualize what you would love to do for the next season of life. If you could design the next season of your life to make good money doing something you love, what would you do? The beauty is there really is no wrong answer. You get to decide what you want to do. And the reality is that there are so many ways to marry passion with profits."

"A lot of dentists assume they can only do one thing. They're programmed to practice dentistry and branded to do only that because others only see them as a dentist, and they only see themselves as a dentist. So, at some point they decide they're done with practicing dentistry and want to do something else. Or, they decide they might not leave dentistry completely but want to start cutting back and start doing a side hustle."

"The key to making any of that successful is to put together a plan and take action. Too many doctors don't know what plan to make, so they have no plan. Years later, they end up selling the practice, retiring, and doing nothing but get bored and old. So many doctors have retired, sold their practice, and there's no life left in them. They start drinking, gambling, or otherwise self-destructing out of a combination of boredom and lack of identity. They don't know who they are once they get out of dentistry. And they have nothing to do all day. They have so much talent, so much incredible brain power, they've accomplished so much, but their identity is a dentist, and that's all they think they are or can be."

I nod. This is so true! But Jerry isn't done yet.

"To me, that's just a bunch of hogwash. The opportunities are limitless if you take action. Look around, start talking to people, find out what's going on, get hooked up with people like Freedom Founders who are creating a better lifestyle after practicing dentistry than they had while practicing. There's so much opportunity, and there's so much to do."

Identity Shift - Finding Your Next

I see that mindset challenge with many doctors who join Freedom Founders. Many join while still practicing. They've been doctors for years. They've been called "Doctor" all day every day. They are so used to being "Doctor" that they have a hard time seeing themselves as more than that. But we're so much more than what we do during the day. We're so much more than our careers. And that's the beauty of being around people like those who are in Freedom Founders. Being in a group of professionals who have been where you are and successfully shifted their mindset—and, ultimately, changed their lives—is powerful. Connecting with people in other businesses, like Jerry did with his dental newsletter company, can change your life.

Just being around people who have left dentistry builds relationships based on empathy, support, and accountability. That's where the chemistry starts to happen—when you get out of the cave of being in the dental office and at the dental chair where all you do is eat, breathe, and speak dentistry, day in and day out. When you're living like that, you can't even begin to think beyond "what you are." When you get out of the office and surround yourself with people who see you for who you are, beyond your degree, you start to see yourself differently and get countless ideas about what you can do during the next season of your life.

The key is to start developing that vision and mindset before it's too late. Make it a part of your practice preparation while you work on cleaning up your finances and operations. That way, you can not only orchestrate a smooth exit but you can also transition smoothly into the next phase of your life.

Bumps In The Road

Finally, we must understand that there will be bumps on the road as we prepare to exit and transition into a newer, more fulfilling season of life. And many times, we're the cause of those bumps. We get in our own way so many times. It's natural given our clinical training, education, and experience. Everything about our clinical care needs to be perfect. We emphasize every detail and obsessively chase perfection to reduce risk. But perfection is not realistic—or even possible. We *will* make mistakes while we prepare our practices for sale. We *will* think we found what we want to move into and learn that it's not what we thought it was.

We need to reign in our instinctive need to compare ourselves to others, but we also need time to focus in on ourselves and explore our options. Sometimes our ideal next is better in theory than it turns out to be in practice. That's just the way it is. All we can do is give ourselves a head start, experiment, and correct course until we find the perfect fit.

You want to get what *you* want out of your life. You don't have to be like everybody else. Try something different. Think differently. Make a commitment to be around people who think differently because that's what's going to help you change your life. It can feel overwhelming to take that first step in a new direction, but you'll never actually take it if you surround yourself with the same people, the same environment, day in and day out, month after month, year after year. But once you put yourself in a position where you can shift your mindset, where you can think outside the box and take the road less traveled, that overwhelming feeling will fade away. It doesn't mean that you'll never make a misstep -- you have to be prepared to have some things not go your way. But you'll just pick back up, adjust and keep forging ahead toward your next, inspired by the exhilaration of freedom.

Takeaways

- Any business, especially a dental practice, needs leadership to create a driven and motivated staff. If becoming an absentee-owner is your exit plan, you forego the cash infusion from a sale and face the potential challenges of a leadership vacuum. If you're looking to get out of dentistry, an outright sale might be the best fit.
- You don't know when it's going to be time to leave, so knowing your exit strategy well in advance is very important. The earlier the better.
- Even if you have the financial means to exit, the biggest challenge of exiting your practice and moving into the next phase of your life is disassociating your sense of identity from your profession. You are much more than a dentist.
- Setbacks teach you a lot as long as you fail fast, adjust, and keep moving forward. A supportive environment can go a long way in helping you take the first step and accelerating the process of exploration.

To listen to the audio recording of my interview with Jerry Jones, go to:
www.SellingYourPracticeBook.com/Interviews

Chapter 8 - Finding—and Funding—Your Next

If you could enter the next phase of your life with financial freedom, moving toward a life of fulfillment and purpose, how would you feel?

Excited? Nervous? Scared?

What would that next phase of your life look like? What would you do if you had the financial freedom and flexibility to design your business and personal life around what *you* want for once?

What would you do?

In 2004, I was faced with a major decision. I had been practicing dentistry for quite some time, working hard to build a successful practice. I had also been investing in real estate since my first year of dental school, 1980, when I convinced my father to buy a two-story brick rental house in Dallas with me. Three years later, we sold the house and split $50,000 in profits. Even better, those profits were capital gains, which meant they were taxed at a much lower rate than earned income.

I was hooked. And as much as I enjoyed practicing dentistry, I wanted to diversify my income, grow my wealth, and position myself to work less than other dentists, and eventually not at all. I had a strong work ethic and didn't mind working long hours. But I didn't want to have all my income dependent on practicing dentistry, so I built enough of a real estate portfolio that I no longer needed to practice to support my family.

But it wasn't until 2004 when a health scare with my twelve-year-old daughter, Jenna, made me realize that while I could do a lot of things to make more *money*, I could not make more *time*. Jenna's childhood had been rough, health-wise: she suffered through intense chemotherapy as a very young girl to fight high-risk leukemia and experienced epileptic seizures from age eight to twelve. Now her liver had failed her, and she received the gift of life in the form of a donor liver.

After Jenna overcame another grueling ordeal--six hours of transplant surgery--I sat by her bedside and started thinking: My practice was successful but stressful, and it added very little value beyond additional income. If anything, it distracted me from the important things in life. So, as I kept asking myself why I continued to practice, I couldn't shake the fact that I just didn't have a good answer.

At that moment, I decided it was time for me to exit dentistry and enter the next phase of my life. My investments would take care of my family financially, and I'd spend my time being with them.

(Today, Jenna is doing very well. She's in college and working toward an associate degree in occupational therapy. She's courageous. She's driven. She's tenacious. She's also a published author and speaker, and she inspires me more than words can express.)

However, after my transition, I quickly realized that the vast majority of dentists wouldn't be able to make the decision I made. That reality hit me hard: I couldn't imagine what it would be like to have been *forced* to continue to practice after Jenna's health scare. Thanks to careful planning and investing, I had the flexibility to focus on my family when they needed me most--but most dentists don't. So I decided to do something about it: my next would be to spend the rest of my professional life helping other dentists reach financial independence, so they can be truly free to live life on their own terms.

The Freedom Formula

Through Freedom Founders, I have helped many dentists build wealth outside of their practices, so they can design and move into the next phase of their life. But money is only half the equation. As I discussed with Jerry Jones, you also need to have a clear plan for what you will be moving *toward* as you exit dentistry.

On the one hand, if you have a clear sense of purpose without financial freedom, you can end up stressed and depressed, chasing a dream with no hope to ever be able to realize it. You would feel stuck, trapped by your need to earn enough to survive, lacking a plan to become financially free. Fortunately, this retirement window gives doctors an opportunity to cash out of dentistry and transition into more passive income models: If your finances and operations are in order, you can do it very quickly; if you need some time to prepare your practice for sale, you're still only a few short years away.

On the other hand, if you build financial freedom by cashing out of dentistry, without also developing a compelling vision for your next phase of life, you can quickly end up unhealthy and unhappy. No matter how much money you have, you need a compelling purpose to be truly free.

Many doctors come to me stuck somewhere in the middle. They have some money saved up. They have some money invested. They have strong income from their dental practice, but they don't want to *have* to earn their income. They don't want to *have* to continue practicing dentistry to fund their lives. With the fear that they are a broken arm or a heart attack away from losing their livelihood, they are not financially free. Without a clear plan for what they want to do next, they're unfulfilled.

Putting together your personal plan—which I like to call "finding your next"—can be challenging, though. We often spend decades focused on working so hard that we don't really develop interests outside of our practices and taking care of our families.

The Danger of Not Knowing Your Next

One of the easiest things to do with a challenging decision is to kick the can down the road. You've practiced dentistry for years. You make good money. You've lived this life every day for the last five, ten, or maybe twenty or thirty years. It feels safe and convenient to leave your course unchanged.

This is the reality for a lot of doctors. They don't know what they want to do next so they do nothing. They're thinking, "I don't know who I'm going to be. I have no place to go. I'll just stay here."

Over time, however, the stress and unhappiness with their practice begin to show up personally and professionally. They let themselves go. They don't work as hard. Their practice slowly declines. By the time they're ready to move on, their practice value has decreased significantly.

During this retirement window with inflated practice values, the impact of indecision is even more pronounced. When—not if—corporate buyers and DSOs are no longer paying a premium for practices, practice values will naturally decline. They will lose their inflated value as well as the value lost as a result of practice decline.

The decision to not search for your next is the equivalent of self-sabotage. You lose the ability to go free not because you *couldn't* become financially free and live your ideal life. You lose it because you *didn't*.

Yes, finances need to be in order. At Freedom Founders, though, we work on finding your next at the same time. We show our members what others have done to achieve freedom, and how they can become more *significant*, and more *empowered* to be leaders in their family, their industry, and their community. We do this through workshops and elite mastermind events designed to get you in the room with me, my team, and experts like the ones you met in this book. That combination gives members a wide variety of information, influence, and support to help them put together their freedom plan.

The Opportunity

It's extremely rare to be able to seize unprecedented opportunities before they pass. With the dental industry, everything I have seen tells me we are in the midst of one of those opportune moments.

But there is only a short window of time during which practice values are inflated and money is pouring into the dental industry--somewhere around three to five more years. Thus, the time is now to find—and fund—a life of greater purpose, passion, and even profits.

Many practitioners get caught in the eternal loop of "paralysis by analysis." They hesitate in uncertainty and choose the "safety" of their current circumstances, even if they are not satisfied or find little meaning in them.

If you are a practitioner in the second half of your career with no exit plan, the time to prepare is now: Optimize your practice to maximize its potential market value; invest time in yourself to start growing as a person beyond dentistry. Begin considering what your "next" might look like. Don't wait.

If you are ready to take the next step toward life after dentistry, visit www.FreedomFounders.com. Our in-person workshops are designed to help you retire earlier and better than you ever dreamed possible. You can get more information about attending on our site.

You can also get more information about our Freedom Founders Elite Mastermind group and apply to secure a guest seat on our site. If you're unfamiliar with masterminds, they are groups of like-minded peers who work together to create economy, solve problems and unleash breakthroughs. Consider it your board of advisors. Whatever your goals or aspirations, a mastermind can exponentially increase your speed to achieve them.

We've helped countless doctors transition into their next with or without selling their practices. So, if you want to experience the same support and accountability that has already helped many others, visit FreedomFounders.com to get started.

No matter how you do it, the time to get started is now!

Claim Your Free Gift From David

A Package Containing Case Studies of Dentists who are Replacing Their Practice Income With Passive Cash Flow.

 You'll receive a book, DVD, and Special Report that share the stories of how real-life dentists "beat the system" and took control of their retirement!

In This Package You Will Discover:

★ Stories of actual practitioners who are **shaving decades off of their retirement timeline.**

★ Why the "4% rule" and traditional retirement planning is FAILING - and what to do instead.

★ The difference between a cash-flow vs accumulation strategy.

★ How to control real estate without the ownership headaches.

To Request Your Free Case Study Package, Go to:
www.FreeGiftFromDavid.com